W9-BUP-776

25 YEARS
F
BUILT to LAST

Playing Together

101 TERRIFIC GAMES AND
ACTIVITIES THAT CHILDREN
AGES 3–9 CAN DO
TOGETHER

Wendy Smolen

A FIRESIDE BOOK
PUBLISHED BY SIMON & SCHUSTER INC.
NEW YORK LONDON TORONTO SYDNEY TOKYO SINGAPORE

FIRESIDE
Rockefeller Center
1230 Avenue of the Americas
New York, NY 10020

FIRESIDE and colophon are registered trademarks
of Simon & Schuster Inc.

Designed by Chris Welch
Illustrated by Jill Weber

Manufactured in the United States of America

1 3 5 7 9 10 8 6 4 2

Library of Congress Cataloging-in-Publication Data
Smolen, Wendy.
Playing together: 101 terrific games and activities that children
ages 3–9 can do together / Wendy Smolen.
p. cm.
"A Fireside book."
Includes index.
1. Games. 2. Indoor games. 3. Creative activities and seat work.
I. Title
GV1203.S634 1995
90.1'922—dc20 95–3527
CIP

ISBN 0-684-80249-X

Dedicated to Dana, Riki, and Zak,
who made me believe in miracles,
and Paul, who makes me believe in myself.

Contents

OUTDOOR GAMES

INDOOR ART PROJECTS

OUTDOOR ART PROJECTS

SEASONAL PROJECTS

Acknowledgments

So many people supported, encouraged, and inspired me while I was writing this book: my parents, my in-laws, my children's teachers, and friends from ages 2 to 82. All deserve special thanks, but to a few I owe even more—Nancy Schulman, Ellen Birnbaum, and Sandra Jenkins who gave me more ideas than I could ever use; Yvette Dorset who made sure that while I was writing, my children *really were* happily playing together; my Dad, who finally figured out how to make the dinner bell work; my incredible editor, Kara Leverte Farley, who, despite the fact that she was having a very real baby, still found the time and energy to nurse me through my own nine months of intensive labor; and finally, my family—Dana, Riki, and Zak, the three in-house testers who can personally vouch for every project that was selected (and could tell you wonderful tales about those that weren't), and Paul, my husband, whom I'd dearly love even if he didn't know how to debug my computer.

introduction

Brothers and sisters. They talk together. They fight. They laugh. They love. And best of all, they play. As the mother of three children between the ages of 3 and 9, I delight in watching the interaction of my kids. But I also cringe when the whining starts, flip if I hear the word "bored," and lose a lot of sleep worrying whether I spend enough time nurturing each child's individual strengths.

By necessity, I've learned how to have "alone time" with all three children at once. Quite simply, I organize one basic activity for everyone. Then, within that activity, I create individual variations by age or skill. In this way, each child can play at his or her own level, all benefit from the others' company, and I can be an active part of the fun.

Playing Together is a collection of the activities that I've found children enjoy regardless of their ages or age differences. Since coordinating several children is complicated enough, the activities I've chosen are intentionally uncomplicated, drawing largely on familiar games, art projects, crafts, and imagination. In most cases, I've used materials that you'll have around the house or that are easy to buy. The general directions apply to all ages; the variations are intended to help you adapt the projects to your particular situation.

As you use the book, please keep in mind that what makes these activities work is their fluidity. In actuality, each one will be as different as your own children. The purpose of *Playing Together* is not to reinvent the wheel, but to enhance the fun of rolling it around.

Enjoy!

Indoor Games

Hide and seek, puppet shows, cards, and treasure hunts. Take the games you loved as a kid, add a little imagination, and you've got a great alternative to the VCR.

Story Bags

Fill a paper bag with stuff and you'll be surprised at what comes out!

MATERIALS

A paper bag for each child

Assortment of odd articles: Try to collect at least five for each bag—for example, a whistle, a scarf, a spoon, a nickel, and sunglasses for one bag.

DIRECTIONS

1. Fill each bag with a varied and unrelated assortment of at least five articles. Close the bags so the children can't see what's inside.
2. Give each child a bag.
3. Have the children look in their bags. Give them a few minutes to think of a story. Then have each child tell a story that uses all of the articles in the bag.

VARIATIONS

3- to 4-Year-Olds

- Work with your child to make up a story. You use one article, he uses the next, you use the third, and so on until all the items are used.

5- to 6-Year-Olds

- Have children work together to make up a play using the articles. Use a different bag of articles for each skit.

7- to 9-Year-Olds

- Have each child make up a play using the articles. Then the child can act it out, playing the different characters and using different voices.

Magazine ABC's

Magazines can be recycled in novel ways. After you've read them, you can cut them, and glue them, and fold them, and use them again and again.

MATERIALS

Magazines: any and all that you don't mind cutting up
Scissors
Glue stick
Paper

DIRECTIONS

1. Choose a magazine and find the letter A. Cut it out.
2. Glue it to a piece of paper.
3. Find a B. Glue it next to the A.
4. Continue through the entire alphabet.

VARIATIONS

3- to 4-Year-Olds

- Do one letter at a time. Find *A*'s all in different sizes and colors. Put them on a single sheet of paper. Do the same with *B* and the remaining letters. It may take weeks, but ultimately you can make an alphabet book by stapling all the pages together.
- Find a terrific A. Or two or three. Glue them to the top of the paper. Find pictures of objects that start with A . . . ants and apples, for example. Cut them out and glue them to the paper. Do the same with *B*. Continue to the end of alphabet.

5- to 6-Year-Olds

- Find all different kinds of *A*'s. Capital ones. Lowercase. Big, small, and script.
- Find *A*'s. Then practice writing *A*'s.
- Write your child's name in cutout letters.

7- to 9-Year-Olds

- Find different letter styles: script, balloon, cartoon, gothic. Try to copy the styles. Have your child make up a type style of his or her own.
- Cut out words and make a short story. Substitute pictures in place of some words to create a rebus.

String Me Along

A combination of hide-and-seek and treasure hunt . . . the prize is your child.

MATERIALS

A large ball of string or yarn for each hider

DIRECTIONS

1. Designate one child as seeker and the rest as hiders. Give each hider a ball of string or yarn.
2. Tie one end of each string to a heavy chair leg. Make a bow, instead of a knot, since it will have to be untied.
3. Each hider takes his or her ball of string and walks around the house, weaving in, out, over, and under furniture and rooms, leaving a string path from the chair leg to his or her eventual hiding place.
4. The seeker unties one string end from the chair. Making a new ball while walking along, the seeker follows the string . . . in, out, over, and under . . . until she or he reaches its hiding owner.
5. The hider now becomes the next seeker. The first seeker becomes a hider.

VARIATIONS

3- to 4-Year-Olds

- If you have more than two children, let the seeker find the first hider and then let the two children work together to find the next hider. That way, all the children will be kept busy, and the strings are less likely to get tangled.

5- to 6-Year-Olds

- Put a treasure at the end of the string instead of a child.
- Let your kids take turns hiding treasures for each other.

7- to 9-Year-Olds

- Make a time limit both for hiding and seeking. Make the seeking time shorter.

Papes

This activity is a personalized version of paper dolls. I remember reading a story about girls who played papes when I was a kid. I recreated the game myself and spent years perfecting it.

MATERIALS

Magazines and catalogs to cut up: Home and fashion magazines make the best papes.
Blank scrapbooks—or make your own by stapling about 12 pages of 8½" x 11" construction paper together at one edge
Scissors
Glue sticks

DIRECTIONS

1. Cut out pictures to make your scrapbook "home." Cut rooms, a house, cars, outdoor areas, anything else you want in your setting. Glue one room or setting on each page in your scrapbook.
2. Cut out a family for your home. Now "dress" them. Instead of cutting out clothes as you would for traditional paper dolls, in papes, you cut out already dressed models. For each person in your papes family, try to find pictures of the same model in different clothes, or other models that look similar.
3. Play papes by moving your family from room to room, changing clothes, making up stories.

VARIATIONS

3- to 4-Year-Olds

- Make a small house, with just a kitchen, children's room, and backyard.

5- to 6-Year-Olds

- Make a school yard and cut out lots of children.

7- to 9-Year-Olds

- Make two families who are neighbors. Create stories about the friendships that develop between them.

Pencil Puppets

One day when my 8-year-old daughter was B-O-R-E-D, she decided to turn her old pencil collection into funny puppets. We've been making pencil puppets ever since.

MATERIALS

Several pencils
Paper
Markers
Scissors
Scotch tape

DIRECTIONS

1. Draw puppet faces on your paper. Use your imagination—make people, animals, monsters, whatever you like. The faces can be from the size of a nickel to the size of a cookie.
2. Cut out your faces and tape them to the eraser ends of pencils. Voila! You have a pencil puppet!

VARIATIONS

3- to 4-Year-Olds

- Put on a puppet show using the kitchen table as a stage.

5- to 6-Year-Olds

- Create a series of puppets that tell a story. Use a familiar fairy tale or a book your children like to read, or make one up.

7- to 9-Year-Olds

- Write a play. Then create the puppets to act in it.
- Dress the puppets with feathers, ribbons, and glitter glue.

HINT

- Round out the puppet cast with any character pencils your children already own (pumpkin pencils from Halloween, Santa pencils, a lollipop-shaped one).

Sardines

This activity is a classic kid's game that's fun for every age. You need a minimum of three to play, but the more, the merrier!

MATERIALS
None

DIRECTIONS

1. Choose one child—or yourself—as the hider. All the rest are the seekers. The hider hides someplace in the house. Designate off-limit rooms if you need to.
2. The seekers start looking. Each seeker who finds the hider joins the hider in the hiding place—squishing into the space like sardines in a can.
3. Play until all the seekers have discovered the hider and are squeezed into the hiding place. The child who found the hider first becomes the hider for the next round.

VARIATIONS

3- to 4-Year-Olds

- Play this game with stuffed animals. Let each child pick a stuffed animal. Have one child hide an animal first. As the children each find the hiding place, they put their animals in the same space. Play until all the animals are hidden. Have a teddy bear picnic for a snack!

5- to 6-Year-Olds

- Play traditional hide-and-seek. All the children hide, and one person seeks. Play till all the children are discovered. The first one to be found is the seeker for the next round. This game even works well with two children.

7- to 9-Year-Olds

- Expand your limits. These kids have the ability to find hiding places where you never thought to look. Give them plenty of room to play.

Freeze Dance

This activity is an updated version of musical chairs—without the chairs! Kids dance when the music is on and "freeze" when it's off. If they move, they're out. The last one left is the winner.

MATERIALS

Tape player: A radio can also be used, but you take your chances with the musical selection.
Upbeat musical tape
Space to dance

DIRECTIONS

1. Turn on the music and watch the kids dance.
2. Quickly turn off the music. The children must freeze in their dance positions.
3. Anyone who moves during the freeze is out.
4. Play until only one child is left.

VARIATIONS

- This is one game all ages play the same way. It helps to gear your choice of music to the oldest children, picking popular tunes that they like to dance to. However, as long as the music is lively, it works.

HINTS

- Adjust your freeze times according to ages—shortest for the shortest kids.
- "Out" players can take turns working the tape player, which is often just as much fun as dancing.

Pitch a Tent

Your children just want to hang out? Take them at their word!

MATERIALS

At least one large blanket or sheet
Heavy books to secure the blanket
Someplace to hang the blanket: I've used a bridge table, the dining room table, four chairs, the top of a bunk bed, the space between two beds.

DIRECTIONS

1. Hang your blanket over the base.
2. Secure the blanket with books or by tucking it in.
3. Bring in your favorite games, and play!

VARIATIONS

3- to 4-Year-Olds

- Play house. Dress up and bring in the stuffed animals. Park the car out front.
- Make two tents and have neighbors.

5- to 6-Year-Olds

- Go camping. Bring flashlights, sleeping bags, and books inside.
- Tell ghost stories and drink from a canteen.

7- to 9-Year-Olds

- Make a "private spot" for reading, or for just getting away from it all.

HINT

- This is a good picnic spot for rainy days.

Memory

Few games cross age lines as easily as Memory. The object of the game is to collect the most two-card matches by remembering where the face-down cards are located. For some reason, in our family, the younger kids always win!

MATERIALS

A deck of cards

DIRECTIONS

1. Spread all the cards out, face down, in four rows of 13 each.
2. The first player turns over two cards. If they match, the player picks them up, puts them in his or her pile, and takes another turn. If they don't match, the player turns them face down again.
3. The next player also turns over two cards, trying to make a match. As more and more cards get exposed, players try to remember where the matches are.
4. When all the pairs have been matched, the person with the biggest pile (or most matches) wins.

VARIATIONS

3- to 4-Year-Olds

- Use only one suit of standard cards for a shorter, easier game.
- Use picture cards, such as Old Maid cards, instead of a standard deck.
- Paste magazine pictures on 3" x 5" index cards. Cut cards in half and make your own memory decks.

5- to 6-Year-Olds

- Use half a deck for a shorter game.
- Fold twenty-six 3" x 5" index cards in half. Write the same letter of the alphabet on both halves of each card. Cut the cards in half, turn them over, and play alphabet memory.

7- to 9-Year-Olds

- Use an egg timer to add an element of excitement.
- Make matches of two red or two black cards of the same numeral.

Shopping Spree

Your children don't think they have enough toys? Let them buy their own! This is a great game to play with different age groups. Just as in the real world, a store is filled with all kinds of shoppers and all kinds of salespeople.

MATERIALS

Merchandise to sell: toys, food, clothes, books, shoes—in other words, whatever you have in quantity!
Display space: This can be the floor, a shelf, bed, sofa.
Shoe box "cash register"
Several shopping bags
Pretend money: Use paper, pasta, marbles, or buttons.
Paper for signs
Crayons

DIRECTIONS

1. Decide what kind of store you want and set up the merchandise for sale.
2. Make price signs out of the paper, and display them next to the goods.
3. Set up your cash register by putting paper money in the shoe box. Cover it. On top of the box draw circles for keys and write the numbers *1* through *10*.
4. Give buyers shopping bags and some money to start. Sellers work the cash register.
5. Shop till you drop!

VARIATIONS

3- to 4-Year-Olds

- Use a toy cash register if you have one instead of a cash box.
- Let the shoppers dress up with a hat, purse, "baby" briefcase. Sellers can create their own "uniform."

5- to 6-Year-Olds

- Make the prices even dollars so children can really count amounts.
- Take turns buying and selling.

7- to 9-Year-Olds

- Use real money. Keep prices low and concentrate on making change!
- Use a calculator instead of a cash register.
- Have an announcer advertise daily specials to the shoppers.

HINTS

- A variation on playing store is playing restaurant. Fold paper into menus, use small pads to write up orders, and serve food to one another or to dolls. Wear an apron or shirt uniform.
- You can make authentic-looking paper money by enlarging the images of dollar bills, front and back, with a photocopier. Use a marker or pencil to color the paper light green. Cut out the bills, and tape the fronts and backs together to make cash.

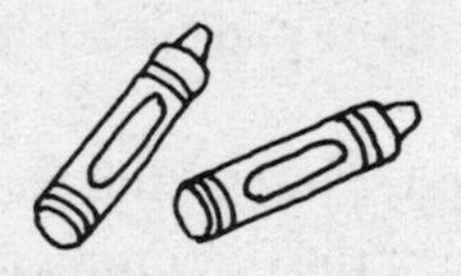

Tic-Tac-Toe

Kids never tire of this classic. It's a two-player game, played on a 9-square grid. The object is to get three *X*'s or three *O*'s in a row. Here, I've jazzed it up with new variations.

MATERIALS

Paper

Pencils or crayons

DIRECTIONS

1. Draw your grid on the paper. The bigger the grid, the easier it is for young ones to play.
2. The first child puts an *X* in a box. The second player puts an *O*.
3. Continue alternating turns until one player aligns three *X*'s or three *O*'s in a row, vertically, horizontally, or diagonally.

VARIATIONS

3- to 4-Year-Olds

- Make a grid with tape in a sticker book, and let children play the game again and again with stickers.
- Use colored circle stickers instead of *X*'s and *O*'s.
- Create a grid on paper and let a child play alone to create his or her own sticker design.

5- to 6-Year-Olds

- Make a 3-D grid with popsicle sticks. (Glue it for keeps.) Play with pennies and nickels.
- Use the children's initials instead of *X*'s and *O*'s.

7- to 9-Year-Olds

- Use a pocket-sized pad so kids can carry the game with them and keep track of scores for a "championship."
- Use graph paper to make the grid easy to draw.

HINT

- When you're playing with a mixed-age group, give the younger child an advantage by letting that child go first. You could also start off by placing the younger child's mark in the center square. It could still be anyone's game—if the second player is clever.

Put On a Happy Face

Talk about emotions and show everyone how you feel.

MATERIALS

Solid-color paper plates
Crayons or markers
Scrap paper

DIRECTIONS

1. Write the words describing common emotions on pieces of scrap paper: "happy," "sad," "angry," "surprised," and so on. Fold the papers and mix them in a pile. Let each child pick an emotion.
2. Have the children illustrate the emotion they picked by drawing a face on their plate using crayons or markers.
3. Ask children to talk about why the face they drew is happy, sad, etc.

VARIATIONS

3- to 4-Year-Olds

- Use geometrically shaped stickers for the eyes or nose, and let the child draw an emotional mouth.
- Turn the plate into a puppet by taping on a tongue depressor handle.
- Make several plates and talk about different feelings.

5- to 6-Year-Olds

- Turn several plates into puppets, and put on a puppet show.
- Make the face a self-portrait, and talk about what makes your child feel certain ways.

7- to 9-Year-Olds

- Draw two plates and have them interact.
- Discuss why a child's plate "feels" a certain emotion and what the child could do to make it feel differently.

Pleasure Hunt

This indoor treasure hunt is an all-around winner. My favorite part is that I always end up finding things that I didn't even realize were missing!

MATERIALS

A treasure: Make it special! It could be new stickers. Or cookies. A gold key ring, a box of neon crayons . . . or several things combined in a gift-wrapped package. You can make a separate treasure for each child, or use one for all.
Paper to write clues
Markers, crayon, or pencil

DIRECTIONS

1. "Bury" your treasure. Hide it in a secret place. Your clues will point the children in the right direction.
2. Write your clues. Each clue will lead to the next, until the last one reveals the hiding place. The more clues you make, the longer the game will last. Try to keep the clues out of the area where the treasure is hidden so no one will "accidentally" find it.
3. Give your child the first clue, and sit back and watch the fun. A typical clue could be:

Look where you go morning and night
To make your teeth sparkling white.

The next clue, hidden by the child's toothbrush, could be:

If it's raining outside and you want to stay dry,
What do you wear so your feet won't cry?

The next clue would be hidden by the child's boots.

Of course, the clues don't have to rhyme and can be harder or easier depending upon your children.

VARIATIONS

3- to 4-Year-Olds

- Make picture clues. In the above example, for the first clue you could draw a toothbrush, shiny teeth, or a tube of toothpaste; for the second clue, rain, boots, or an umbrella and raincoat.

5- to 6-Year-Olds

- Make word games. For example:

You comb your hair and b______ your teeth.
An owl hoots. In the rain, you wear b______.

7- to 9-Year-Olds

- After you make a treasure hunt, have your child make one for you or another child to follow.

Sock-it-to-Me Puppet Show

Here's a purpose for all your unmatched socks.

MATERIALS

Old socks, preferably light-colored
Colored markers
Puppet stage area: The back of a sofa is ideal. A bridge table or large chair also works.

DIRECTIONS

1. Lay the sock out flat. Draw a vertical line about an inch in from the toe, and a horizontal line about an inch up from the bottom, extending from heel to toe. Turn the sock over and do the same thing on the other side.
2. Color in the entire drawn frame with markers. This will become your puppet's mouth.
3. Make an eye on the part of the sock that would normally be covered by your shoelaces. Turn the sock over and make a second eye on the other side.
4. Put the sock on your hand, using your thumb in one section and the rest of your fingers in another to make your puppet talk.
5. Hide behind a sofa or high table, and let your puppet perform for the audience.

VARIATIONS

3- to 4-Year-Olds

- Put a Band-Aid strip on one finger of your other hand. Draw a face on it and make that your puppet's friend. Let the two puppets have a conversation.

5- to 6-Year-Olds

- Sell tickets to the puppet show.
- Make a playbill.
- Have music.
- Draw on more puppet details, such as ears or a nose.
- Glue on yarn for hair.

7- to 9-Year-Olds

- Write a play for the puppets to perform. Make different types of puppets to fit each part.

HINT

- While the older children are writing their play, there's still plenty for the younger ones to do: cut out tickets; draw a play-bill, and make signs. They can also be the ones to collect tick-ets and announce the play.

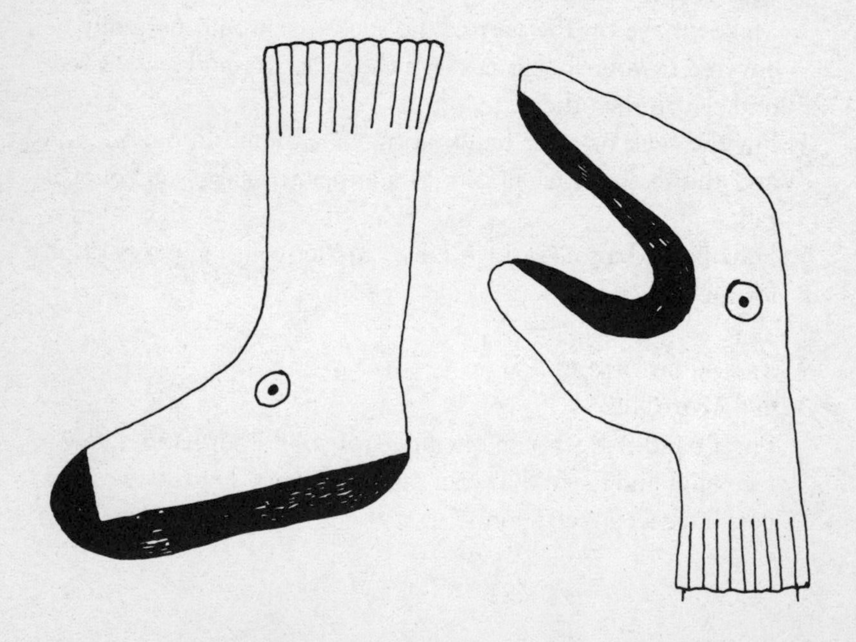

I Love a Parade

Even better, my kids love a parade!

MATERIALS

Costumes: hats, batons, cowboy boots, tutus, and similar items
Something you can pull for a float: an indoor wagon, a toddler's pull toy, a car on a string, or a shoe box on a ribbon
Musical instruments such as drums, triangles, horns, and bells
A tape recorder and marching music tapes

DIRECTIONS

1. Announce a theme for your parade. Is it a Fourth of July, a Christmas, a Rose Bowl, or even a "Rainy Tuesday" celebration?
2. Plan costumes around the theme. This is half of the fun. Let children use their imaginations to dress up for their parts.
3. Let each child design a float to pull. If you have indoor wagons or riding toys, these can be decorated. Otherwise, use pull toys or take a shoe box, fit it with dolls or other toys, and staple a ribbon on it for pulling.
4. Turn on the music tapes, grab a musical instrument, gather the props, and march!

VARIATIONS

3- to 4-Year-Olds

- Make an animal parade. Line up the stuffed animals, and have them march to the zoo.
- Make an animal caravan by putting stuffed animals in shoe boxes and connecting the boxes with ribbon. You lead the way by pulling the first "car."

5- to 6-Year-Olds

- Make different kinds of floats for the dolls.
- Use toy cars for the police and for celebrities.

7- to 9-Year-Olds

- Make elaborate drum major, band, or soldier uniforms.
- Practice marching in step to some music.
- Come up with original ideas for decorated floats.

HINT

- You can also play Stop-Go with the music tapes. Have the kids march around. Turn off the music and they must *stop.* Turn it on and they go.

War

Forget the name. This classic card game has kept peace in my house for years. It takes more luck than skill, so as long as your children can count, they can play.

MATERIALS

A deck of playing cards

DIRECTIONS

1. Deal the entire deck. If two are playing, each gets 26 cards; if three, then two get 17, one gets 18. Everyone keeps the cards in a separate pile.
2. All players turn over their top card. Whoever has the highest card gets to take all the other upturned cards.
3. If two players turn over the same value card at the same time (for example, two queens), they have a "war." The players leave the queens face up. They take the next top three cards in their piles and place the cards face down in a line. (I call these the "W," "A," "R" cards.) Finally, they take a fourth card and place it face up at the end of the line. Whoever has the highest-value fourth card wins the entire collection of outlaid cards.
4. Players continue playing through the entire deck. The person whose pile is biggest at the end of the round, wins.

VARIATIONS

3- to 4-Year-Olds

- Play with half a deck.
- Take out the jacks, queens, and kings, or make them all the same value.
- Play your own game, matching the cards by color, number, and suit.

5- to 6-Year-Olds

- Don't play just one round! Keep playing until one person runs out of cards.

7- to 9-Year-Olds

- Add the jokers into the deck and make them wild cards.
- Learn to play solitaire; there are dozens of variations.

HINT

- Any number can play War. You can also play in teams, pairing the youngest with the oldest to help with the counting.

Outdoor Games

Did you ever notice how happy everyone is outside? Whether your backyard is grass or gravel, a park, a pavement, a block, or a beach, kids instinctively know: The sky's the limit to how high they can jump, how fast they can run, and how loud they can yell.

Sunny Day Tic-Tac-Toe

It's a race against the sun when you play tic-tac-toe with water. Like so many simple games, this was invented on the spur of the moment—by Sandra Jenkins, Dana's third-grade teacher.

MATERIALS

Pail of water
A paintbrush for each child
A sunny flagstone surface or cement sidewalk
Sidewalk chalk

DIRECTIONS

1. Draw a large tic-tac-toe grid on your flagstone with chalk. This is where the children play classic tic-tac-toe . . . with water.
2. The first child draws an *X* in a box using a paintbrush and water.
3. The second child draws an O.
4. Continue playing until someone wins by getting three *X*'s or *O*'s in a row. The trick is to go quickly—before the sun dries your mark and frees that square for your opponent.

VARIATIONS

3- to 4-Year-Olds

- Paint patterns in the squares and watch them disappear.
- Paint your child's name in water.
- Make chalk drawings and drip water on them to create new designs.

5- to 6-Year-Olds

- Paint pictures in water and see how long they last. Time them either using a stop watch or by racing two children against each other.
- Instead of X's and O's, come up with other watermarks. A solid block will last a long time. How about stripes or dots?

7- to 9-Year-Olds

- Make the rules stricter. If water gets on the chalk grid, the player loses a turn.
- Can you also make the grid out of water?
- Is there a difference between how long the X's and O's last?

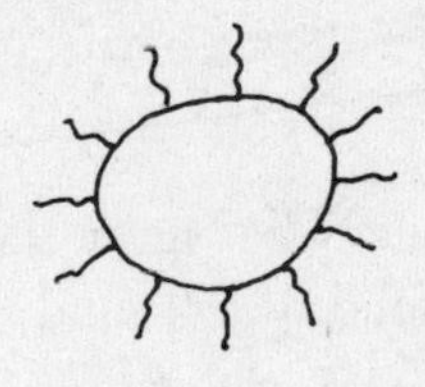

Build a Sand Matterhorn

Better than a sand castle, easier than a ski slope, it's a sand slope. Look out below!

MATERIALS

Sand, in a sandbox or at the beach
A tennis ball or small jacks ball—one for each child, if possible
Water if the sand is very dry

DIRECTIONS

1. Build a huge sand pile. The bigger, the better.
2. Pat the pile so it's solid. If the sand is too dry, add water so it stays in place.
3. Place one ball on the top of the pile. Now make a path for the ball to roll down: Gently roll the ball around and around the pile, spiraling down to the bottom. After you've gently drawn your path, do it again, with more pressure so the path is deep enough so the ball stays in it.
4. Place the ball at the top of the pile again and push it. It should speed down the mountain! (If it doesn't, correct any trouble spots by making your path steeper.)

VARIATIONS

3- to 4-Year-Olds

- Use the paths to run small trucks or trains up and down the mountain.
- Retell the story of *The Little Engine That Could* as you move the ball up the mountain and watch it go down.

5- to 6-Year-Olds

- Make a water hole at the bottom of the mountain to catch the ball.
- Make two piles about the same size. Have races.

7- to 9-Year-Olds

- Make tunnels along the path that the ball can go through.
- Make a very large pile and create two paths to race balls. Try to make them equal lengths.

Puddle Walks

Nothing's more fun than walking in water! As simple as this sounds, it's a great energy releaser.

MATERIALS

Rain boots
Rain puddles

DIRECTIONS

1. Put on the boots.
2. Walk outside with the exclusive purpose of splashing in the puddles.

VARIATIONS

3- to 4-Year-Olds

- Bring a boat to sail.

5- to 6-Year-Olds

- Play follow the leader. As the children wander from puddle to puddle, the leader skips, jumps, or hops through the water.

7- to 9-Year-Olds

- Toss small stones into the puddle and watch the ripples.
- See who can jump the farthest . . . over or into the puddle.

HINT

- If it's warm enough, do this barefoot.

Shadow Puppets

Have a built-in playmate on a sunny day!

MATERIALS

Your hands
A sidewalk
The sun

DIRECTIONS

1. Position yourself so the sun shines over your back and you can see your shadow.
2. Make puppets using your hands. The simplest animal can be made by touching your thumb to the middle of your other four fingers (as though you were wearing mittens). Add ears by raising the index and the middle fingers.
3. Make your puppets talk by moving your fingers.

VARIATIONS

3- to 4-Year-Olds

- Hold your hand open flat to make a hand puppet. Watch the shadow when you wiggle your fingers.
- Make your shadow and your child's touch without touching each other in real life.

5- to 6-Year-Olds

- Create different shadow animals by raising or bending fingers, or by using two hands.
- See how big or small you can make your shadows.

7- to 9-Year-Olds

- See what happens to the shadow when the sun is in front of you, or at your side.
- Make a shadow puppet show.

Sprinkle, Sprinkle

It's hard to remember that the object here is *not* to get wet!

MATERIALS

Rotating lawn sprinkler, either back-and-forth or revolving
Hose and water connection
Lawn to be watered!

DIRECTIONS

1. Hook up the sprinkler and turn on the water.
2. Make two end zones where the water doesn't reach.
3. As the water revolves, let the children run back and forth between end zones trying not to get wet.

VARIATIONS

3- to 4-Year-Olds

- Turn the water on low so it doesn't spray as hard and fast.
- Let kids wear raincoats.

5- to 6-Year-Olds

- Work in teams. Have a child in each end zone. One yells "Go" and they both run at the same time.

7- to 9-Year-Olds

- Put an object near the sprinkler. The child has to pick it up and bring it back to the end zone without getting (too) wet.
- Make relay teams using two objects. On each team, one child picks up the object and the next child puts it back.

Have a Potluck Picnic

Any season, any reason, food always tastes better at a picnic!

MATERIALS

Food
Drinks
Paper plates and cups
Plastic silverware
Napkins
Tablecloth
Trash bag

DIRECTIONS

1. Decide what and where you're going to eat. Breakfast at the beach is as good as dinner under the stars. Lunch in the park is an easy treat. In the same vein, there's no rule against tuna fish for breakfast, muffins for lunch, or apples for hors d'oeuvres.
2. Assign courses. Each child should pick out one food. Have hors d'oeuvres, entrees, dessert, nibbles, drinks.
3. Make it. Pack it. Eat it.
4. Clean up by tossing everything in your trash bag.

VARIATIONS

3- to 4-Year-Olds

- Someone has to count the napkins, plates, and silverware!

5- to 6-Year-Olds

- Collect table decorations such as outdoor candles, flowers, even rocks to keep the napkins from blowing.

7- to 9-Year-Olds

- Wrap the sandwiches. Pack finger foods in plastic containers or bags.

HINTS

- Make your food fun! Chocolate milk, sandwiches shaped with cookie cutters, baggies full of ready-to-eat grapes, carrot curls (cut strips, roll them up, secure with a toothpick, and soak overnight in cold water), or melon balls—all can be prepared by the kids.
- Pack outdoor equipment such as balls, mitts, and jump ropes.
- A picnic can also be a barbeque. Grilling outside is easy for you and fun for kids. Don't forget the marshmallows!

Go Fishing

If you're lucky enough to live by water, fishing is a wonderful way to spend the day. But even when you're inland, you can still cast a line.

MATERIALS

A strong, thick stick for the pole
String
Paper clips for hooks
Small magnets for bait
Kiddie pool or large tub of water
Objects to catch: paper clips, scarves, empty cans, coins, sunglasses, and keys

DIRECTIONS

1. Make your pole. Tie string on one end of the pole. Uncurl a paper clip halfway. Tie it on the other end of the string for your hook. Attach a small magnet near the clip for bait.
2. Fill the pool with a few inches of water and a variety of "fishy" objects.
3. Try to catch them!

VARIATIONS

3- to 4-Year-Olds

- Go balloon fishing. Blow up several balloons. Attach a half opened paper clip to the knotted end of each balloon. Try to hook the fish with the rod and magnet bait.

5- to 6-Year-Olds

- Do balloon fishing (as above). Instead of using magnets, try to hook balloons with the paper clip hook.
- Try fishing with a blindfold.

7- to 9-Year-Olds

- Make it a contest. Who can catch the most fish? The biggest fish? The smallest one?
- Have a pollution lesson. What can't be caught and stays at the bottom of the pond? If you run out of bait, is there another way to get objects, like using two sticks, chopstick-style, to pick up a can?

HINT

- You can also do this activity with no water in the tub.
- The objects to catch should be lightweight. Use a variety of metallic and nonmetallic things. The magnets will easily pick up the metals, but you may be able to "hook" some of the others.

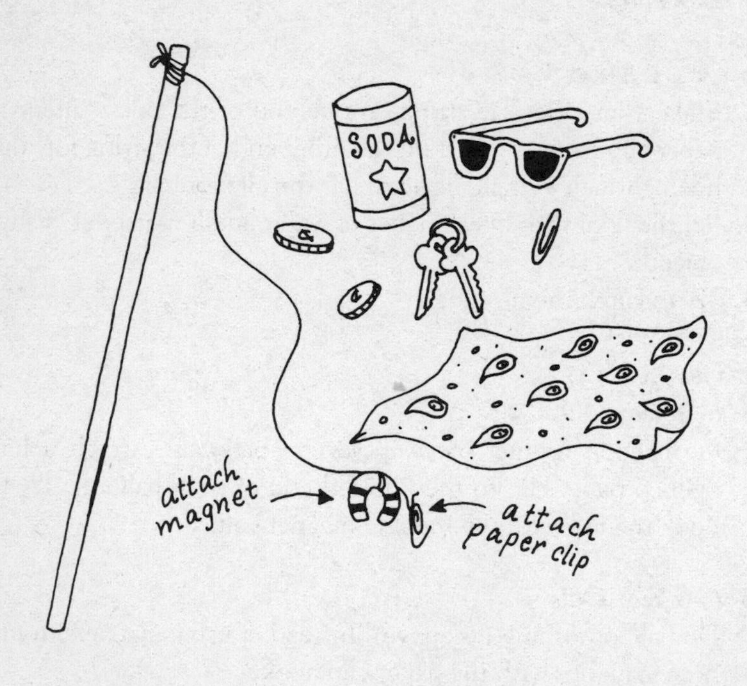

Over, Under, Around, and Through

Let your kids run wild! An obstacle course will keep them within bounds.

MATERIALS

A large play area

Anything you can find to run over, under, around, or through: lawn chairs, boxes, an empty kiddie pool, a hose, a tree

DIRECTIONS

1. Define your play area.
2. Set up your course in a logical manner. Remember, your kids will be running through it, so they need to be able to follow an easy sequence.
3. Alternate the faster activities, such as running, with slower ones, such as jumping. This will keep the action under control. A sample course could be:

   Jump down three porch steps, one at a time.
   Run across the lawn to touch the garden gate.
   Crawl through an empty box.
   Walk through a spiral maze created by a garden hose.
   Hop to the swing set.
   Swing on your tummy four times.
   Run backwards around the lawn chairs.
   Twirl back to the porch.

VARIATIONS

3- to 4-Year-Olds

- If hopping, walking backwards, or any other activities are too hard, or too hard to remember in sequence, let children run through the whole course.

5- to 6-Year-Olds

- Make it a race. Children start at opposite ends.

7- to 9-Year-Olds

- Use a stopwatch. Have children race against each other or against the clock.

HINTS

- Your course will vary with the age of your children and your available obstacles. Let the kids help plan it—and let it evolve over several days.
- If your children have a lot of friends visiting, you can turn the course into a relay race. Make two teams of combined ages, and have the children start at different "posts" along the route.

Treasure Island

This can be a team game—with the pirates who bury the treasure and the explorers who find it.

MATERIALS

Paper and pencils for a map

A treasure: It can be anything from pennies in a jar to a collection of sparkling rocks. Just remember, it's going to be "buried" outdoors.

DIRECTIONS

1. Decide which children will be the pirates who bury the treasure and make the map and which will be explorers who find it. If you make teams, combine age groups. The little kids can help hide or dig; the older kids can draw the maps.
2. Find or make a treasure.
3. Hide it outside. It doesn't have to be actually buried . . . just well hidden.
4. Help pirates make a treasure map of your yard.
5. Put an X where the treasure is.
6. Let the explorers find the treasure.

VARIATIONS

3- to 4-Year-Olds

- Draw your map with footprints showing where to walk to find the treasure.
- Draw a blank map and let children mark where they want to put the treasure. Then let them put it there.

5- to 6-Year-Olds

- Let children draw their own maps, bury a treasure, and mark it on the map. Put the map in an envelope and save the "exploration" for another day's activity.

7- to 9-Year-Olds

- Show north, east, south, and west on the map. Write instructions for where to find the treasure using those directions. Let children use a compass. Sample instructions could be:

> *Walk north from the garage; turn west at the hedge;*
> *walk 4 yards and turn south.*

HINT

- If everyone wants to be an explorer, you can be the pirate and bury the treasure yourself.

Giant Slalom Course

This one's a winner for everybody because it has so many variations. Once you set up a course, the only limits are your children's own ability level.

MATERIALS

6 or 8 plastic cones: These look like the orange kind you see at construction sites, but they're scaled down to kid size. If you don't have cones, any kind of low, indestructible marker will do. I've used plastic mixing bowls, weighted pie tins, and upside down sand pails.

An open yard or safe driveway

DIRECTIONS

1. Set up the cones in a line. Space them far enough apart so that there's room to run, hop, skip, and jump around each one. The farther apart they are, the easier.
2. Create start and finish lines.
3. Decide what kind of slalom it is: running, skipping, hopping, or jumping.
4. Have children start at one end and weave their way back and forth through the cones (doing the activity you've selected) until they come to the finish line.

VARIATIONS

3- to 4-Year-Olds

- Let children practice a new skill, such as skipping. Try to go from start to finish without missing a beat.

- Have children pretend to be an airplane, flying through the course. Let them make up other things they could be: a butterfly, a rabbit, a dog, the wind.

5- to 6-Year-Olds

- Let children make up ways to go through the course with a partner: such as a wheelbarrow walk or leap frog.
- Start the children at opposite sides, and let them race.

7- to 9-Year-Olds

- Let children roller-skate, jump-rope, or skateboard through the course.
- Have children kick a soccer ball through the course.

Kids' Croquet

Make up new rules for this old-time lawn game.

MATERIALS

A croquet set: 4 mallets; 4 balls; 10 wickets.

DIRECTIONS

1. Set up the wickets in a progressive pattern, spacing each one several feet from the previous one.
2. Give each child a mallet and ball.
3. Let children take turns trying to hit their ball through each wicket.

VARIATIONS

3- to 4-Year-Olds

- Set up rows of three or four wickets each. Have children hit the balls through those.
- Let children roll the balls through the wickets instead of using mallets.

5- to 6-Year-Olds

- Set up two rows of five wickets each. Space the wickets about a foot apart. Have the children try to hit the ball so it goes through all five wickets.
- Set up two patterns of five wickets. Make it a race to see who can hit the ball through each wicket in his or her pattern.

7- to 9-Year-Olds

- Let children play like miniature golf. Set wickets in patterns—around trees, near sand, etc. Keep score by adding the number of strokes it takes to get the ball through each wicket. The lowest score wins.
- Place one ball about 10 feet away. Have children stand behind a line and roll their ball to try to hit the "master" ball. If no one can hit it, the one who gets closest, wins.

Jumping for Joy

Jump rope isn't only a girls' playground game; boys, little kids, and grown-ups can play too.

MATERIALS

A long jump rope or clothesline
A shorter, single-person jump rope

DIRECTIONS

1. Have two people hold the ends of the long jump rope. Or tie one end of the rope to a tree or fence or heavy outdoor chair, and have one person hold the other end. Twirl the rope.
2. Let children take turns running into the twirling rope to jump. If that's too hard, have the child stand next to the rope and have the end people begin their twirling with the child already in place.
3. Count or chant a rhyme as the child jumps.

VARIATIONS

3- to 4-Year-Olds

- Try using a short jump rope. Remind the children: It takes practice.
- Lay the rope flat on the ground, and let children try to tightrope-walk across it.

5- to 6-Year-Olds

- Play limbo with the long rope. Have two people hold it up as high as they can. All the children walk under it. After all have had a turn, lower the rope. Repeat the process. Children must bend *backwards* as they walk under the rope . . . never touching it. If they touch it, they're out. Keep playing to see how low they can go.
- Practice using a short rope.

- Put on your children's favorite tape and let them jump to the music.

7- to 9-Year-Olds

- Have contests with long or short ropes to see who can jump the most.
- Encourage children to learn new jump rope chants to sing with friends. See if you remember any!
- Use two long ropes and have children jump double Dutch.
- Get children to do tricks . . . turn around, go on one foot, touch a toe.

HINT

- Team up your kids and use the rope for a great game of tug-of-war.

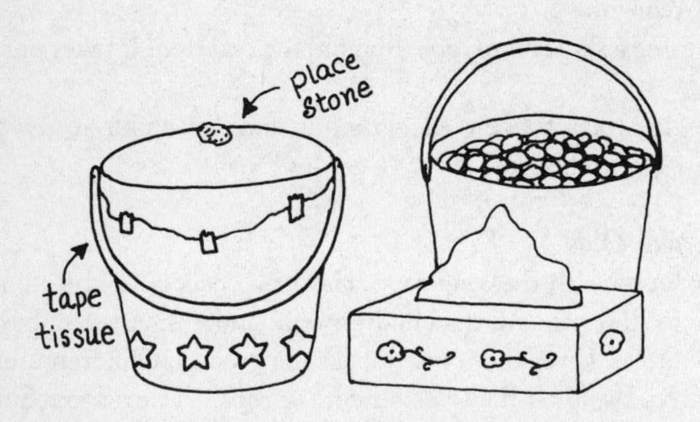

See "Look Out Below!" on the next page.

Look Out Below!

Water, stones, action! This game has something for everyone.

MATERIALS

20 stones of varying sizes—small driveway stones work best.
An empty sand pail
A second pail, containing water
Box of tissues
Scotch tape

DIRECTIONS

1. Lay one tissue over the sand pail, and tape it to the edges as tight as you can.
2. Put your stones in the second pail, filled with water.
3. One at a time, each child takes a wet stone and places it on the tissue, trying not to let the stone break through the paper.
4. The child whose stone finally breaks through is out and has to set up the pail again for the next game.

VARIATIONS

3- to 4-Year-Olds

- Use two tissues at a time to make the surface stronger and make the game last longer.

5- to 6-Year-Olds

- Let a child play solitaire; count how many stones she or he can gently lay on the tissue without breaking it.

7- to 9-Year-Olds

- Make a series. Spell the word "stone." Whoever breaks the tissue first gets an *S*. If the same child breaks the tissue in the next game, he or she gets a *T*, and so on. Whoever spells "stone" first is out. Play until only one child is left.

Playing for Peanuts

What to do when there's nothing to do? Look for peanuts. Inevitably, not every one is going to be found . . . and you may sight peanuts for days afterwards.

MATERIALS

A bag of peanuts
A small empty bag or basket for each child

DIRECTIONS

1. Hide the peanuts all over your yard. Just make sure they're in places children can safely reach.
2. Explain the boundaries to your children. Give each child a bag, and then let everyone hunt for peanuts.
3. Whoever has the most peanuts, wins.

VARIATIONS

3- to 4-Year-Olds

- Work in teams.

5- to 6-Year-Olds

- Work against the clock. Whoever has the most nuts after 10 minutes wins. The winner can set up the game again.

7- to 9-Year-Olds

- If you have a food scale, weigh your nuts. Whoever has the heaviest bag of nuts, wins. The largest number of nuts isn't necessarily the heaviest. Before weighing, children can trade nuts . . . two smalls for one large, and so on.

HINT

- If you're playing with a group of children with a wide range of ages and abilities, color-code your nuts. Take a magic marker and make a red mark for the youngest kids, blue for middle, black for oldest. Hide the red nuts in the lowest, easiest spots; blue next; black hardest. The children can only gather the nuts marked with their color.

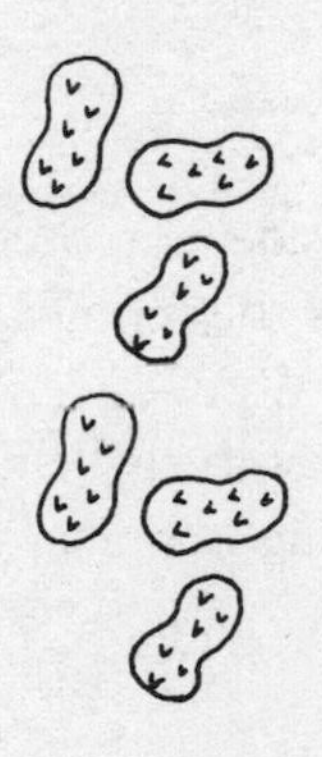

Penny Bounce

I learned this game from Ellen Birnbaum, a fabulous nursery school teacher who says she spent years of her childhood playing it. Once you try it, you'll understand why!

MATERIALS

A few pennies
A tennis ball

DIRECTIONS

1. Place a penny on the sidewalk. Step back about 3 feet.
2. The first player tosses the tennis ball, trying to hit the penny and make it bounce.
3. The next player catches the ball and takes a turn.
4. Keep score by counting how many times each child hits the penny.

VARIATIONS

3- to 4-Year-Olds

- Use a larger playground ball.
- Have children kneel down and bounce the ball towards the penny.

5- to 6-Year-Olds

- Work as a team. Draw a large circle around the penny with chalk. Take turns throwing the ball to see if you can get the penny to bounce out of the circle. Use more balls if you want, so each child can have one.

- Draw a large square around the penny. One person stands on one side; the other person stands on the opposite side. Try to bounce the penny across to the opponent's side. Use two balls if you want.

7- to 9-Year-Olds

- Start 3 feet away from the penny. Every time you hit it, move back a step.
- Have a penny race. Make start and finish lines, and bounce the penny to make it "run."

Bean Bag Toss

If your kids like to throw things, try a bean bag. It can't hurt. Can't break. And you can't stop playing!

MATERIALS

A bean bag for each child: Buy them, or make your own by sewing dried beans in a square of fabric.

Something to throw them in: bowls, pails, or pots

DIRECTIONS

1. Set the bowls on the ground about 6 feet away from the children.
2. Have the children stand behind a line and try to toss the bean bags into the bowls.

VARIATIONS

3- to 4-Year-Olds

- Move the bowls closer if the child can't do it.
- Use a large tub instead of a bowl or pail.
- Play catch. Bean bags are easier than balls.

5- to 6-Year-Olds

- Take a break from tossing and have children race with bean bags balanced on their heads. If the bean bag falls off, the child has to start again.
- Make a target with chalk and see how close the child can get to the bull's-eye.

7- to 9-Year-Olds

- Put the bowls on a table and have children try to toss the bags in.
- Have children throw overhand.
- Have children throw with their opposite hand.

HINT

- Make a clown face bean bag toss out of a large packing box. Cut a hole in one side and have children paint a face around the hole. Let children try to toss the bag into the mouth! This is a great party game.

Indoor Art Projects

To me, craft supplies are as basic as peanut butter and jelly. I always keep an ample supply on hand and can whip them out at any time to satisfy just about everybody. I am never without a stack of magazines, pipe cleaners, clear contact paper, stickers, construction paper, crayons, markers, and craft glue. I also hoard collage materials in a huge plastic storage box: birthday ribbons and wrapping paper scraps, feathers, tissue paper, cotton, foil, sequins, doilies, and anything else that's colorful, fuzzy, and fun!

Handprints

Today's handprints are tomorrow's fossils. I've created a time tunnel by hanging them in a hallway.

MATERIALS

Modeling clay—the kind that hardens
Waxed paper
Bowl, approximately 6 inches in diameter
Rolling pin
Toothpick or juice box straw
Ribbon or cord for hanging

DIRECTIONS

1. Start with a large ball of soft clay. Roll it on top of the waxed paper to be about 8" x 8" in size and ½-inch thick.
2. Lay the child's hand flat in the center of the clay and press down to create an impression.
3. Press the bowl upside down over the handprint like a cookie cutter. Trim the excess clay from around the bowl and then remove the bowl. You should be left with one print in a flat circle of clay.
4. Wet your fingers and smooth the edges of your circle.
5. Poke a small hole in the top on the circle using the toothpick or straw.
6. Carve the child's name and the date in the clay with the toothpick.
7. Let the print dry overnight on the waxed paper. String a ribbon or cord through the hole for hanging.

VARIATIONS

3- to 4-Year-Olds

- Make footprints. Kids think this is a riot!
- Paint the finished piece.

5- to 6-Year-Olds

- While the clay is wet, decorate the outside of the handprint with buttons.
- Sponge-paint the finished piece.

7- to 9-Year-Olds

- Add "jewelry" to the print. Make a clay ring or bracelet. Add beads or sequins for jewels.

HINTS

- We do this project around the same time every year so we can see how everyone's hands have grown.
- You may want to make Mommy and Daddy prints to complete your collection.
- Kids love the feel of clay. Let them squish it between their fingers and poke, pound, and roll it while you organize the main steps of this project.

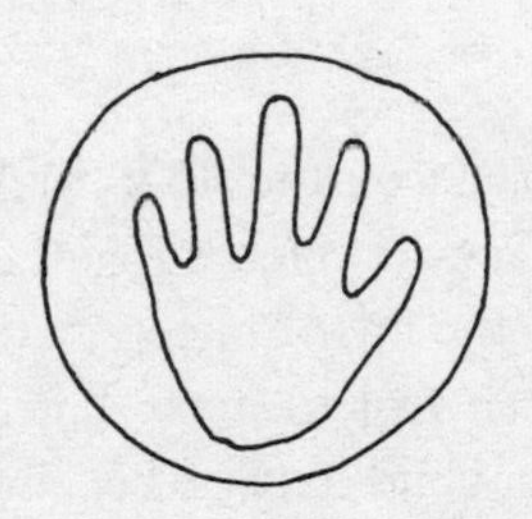

Self-Portraits

You'll be surprised how children really see themselves!

MATERIALS

A large roll of brown craft paper or several heavy grocery bags for each child
Crayons and markers
Scissors
Masking tape
Glue stick
Yarn for hair

DIRECTIONS

1. Spread the craft paper on the floor. Make it longer and wider than your child. Tape two pieces together if you need to. Tape the entire piece to the floor to keep it still. If you use shopping bags, cut them open first to make flat pieces. You'll probably need about four per child to get a big enough expanse of paper. Put the smoother sides face down, and tape the sides that have folds and extra layers. This will become the back of your figure.
2. Have your child lie face up on top of the paper, arms just slightly extended and legs slightly separated.
3. With a crayon or marker, trace your child's shape.
4. Cut out the shape, turn it over, and tape it to the floor or a mat to keep it from moving.
5. Have your child draw a self-portrait inside the shape, starting with the face. Cut yarn for the hair and use the glue stick to paste it on.

6. Let the child "dress" the figure by drawing a favorite outfit . . . including shoes.
7. Remove the floor tape and hang the figure in a prominent place.

VARIATIONS

3- to 4-Year-Olds

- Use collage materials for designer clothes.

5- to 6-Year-Olds

- Use construction paper to cut out clothes and dress the figure.
- Create several outfits for human-sized paper dolls.

7- to 9-Year-Olds

- Create joints on the figure: Cut off the arms and legs, and then cut them each in half (at the elbow and knee). Reattach the pieces to the body with paper fasteners. Pose the figure by bending the arms and legs.

HINT

- You can do this project using heavy cardboard, such as from a packing box, or poster board. It's harder to cut—use a mat knife—but the figure will be stiff enough to actually dress in your child's own clothing.

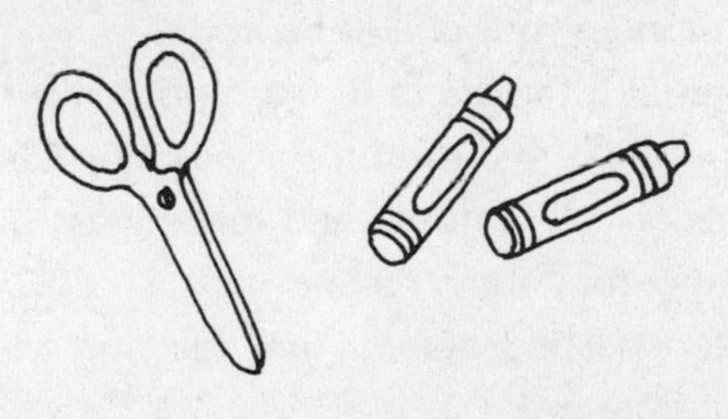

Dioramas

A diorama is a scene you create inside a box. It can be totally imaginary or a replica of a real place. But no matter what you make, it's your own perfect world.

MATERIALS

A shoe box
Glue and tape
Magazines to cut up
Construction paper
Small figures, cars, or other objects your child wants to create a home for
Crayons or markers
Scissors
Cellophane wrap
Any colorful, unusual scraps of paper or material you have handy: aluminum foil, wrapping paper, cellophane, netting, tissue paper, cotton

DIRECTIONS

1. Help your child decide what the diorama theme will be. Will you make a seashore scene, outer space, a jungle, a highway, a classroom, or even your child's bedroom?
2. Gather materials that would be appropriate for that theme. For example, use shells and sand for a seashore. Or cut out magazine pictures of wild animals and make grass from green construction paper for a jungle scene.
3. Stand the open shoe box on its side and visualize how to arrange you diorama.
4. Before you start to paste, do any coloring you want. It's a lot easier to move your hands around the box when there is nothing else inside.

5. Arrange your materials and glue them in place. Consider using cotton for clouds, cellophane for water, aluminum foil for mirrors, and folded paper for chairs, tables, and other furniture.
6. Let the diorama dry; place any figurines or objects inside.
7. Protect the scene by taping cellophane wrap over the box opening.

VARIATIONS

3- to 4-Year-Olds

- Make a diorama of a place your child frequents, such as a playground. Gather materials from the area to use in the scene.

5- to 6-Year-Olds

- Make a fantasy scene rather than a real one.
- Create a diorama of a favorite story.

7- to 9-Year-Olds

- Picture history lessons, the solar system, or a holiday setting.

Magnetic Attractions

You can never have too many refrigerator magnets.

MATERIALS

A roll of stick-on magnetic tape: You can buy it at a hardware store.
Foam board or heavy cardboard, such as from a box
A picture of your child
Scissors
Glue stick
Clear contact paper

DIRECTIONS

1. Cut the foam board or cardboard into shapes (circles, squares, rectangles, etc.), each about 2 to 3 inches wide.
2. Using the glue stick, glue the photo onto the foam board.
3. Trim the photo to be the shape of the foam board.
4. Cut a piece of clear contact paper about ½ inch bigger than your design. Place the design face down on the sticky side of the contact paper, and wrap the excess paper around the back of the foam board. This will protect the photo as you handle it again and again.
5. Cut the magnetic strip into inch-long pieces. Peel off the protective paper from the sticky side and press the magnet onto the back of the foam board.
6. Stick the magnet onto your refrigerator!

VARIATIONS

3- to 4-Year-Olds

- Paint or color the magnets instead of gluing on photos.
- Cut out magazine photos and make a magnet zoo . . . or highway . . . or magnet foods.

5- to 6-Year-Olds

- Make magnet letters to write your child's name. Cut the letters from magazines and glue them on.

7- to 9-Year-Olds

- Make "designer" magnets using collage materials.
- Make real food magnets by gluing on rice, beans, peas, or small pieces of pasta.

Mobiles

These mobiles are so much fun, I always make one myself!

MATERIALS

A large piece of corrugated cardboard, at least 12" x 12". (It doesn't have to be square.)
Ribbon or string
Materials to hang: paper, shells, beads, feathers, colored cellophane, tiny figures, and the like
Sharp scissors
Optional: tape and stapler

DIRECTIONS

1. Cut the cardboard into a spiral. Start at one end, about 3 inches in from the corner. Work your way up the longest side, cutting around and around. Try to keep your "circles" about 3 inches wide so they'll be strong enough to support the mobile. When you reach the center, leave a fist-sized area to be the top of the mobile.
2. Using the sharp end of the scissors, poke a hole in the center area. Put a string or ribbon through the hole, leaving a long piece at the top for attaching to the ceiling. Knot the other end.
3. Poke several other holes at random intervals among the spiral. Put pieces of string in these holes, knotting them at the top, with the long sides down. These will hold your mobile objects.
4. Tie the objects onto the strings. You may want to tape or staple the lighter materials instead of tying. Help your child balance the mobile by putting heavier materials at the top of the spiral.
5. Find a high hook to hang it on, and your mobile is complete!

VARIATIONS

3- to 4-Year-Olds

- A simpler mobile can be made using a wire hanger. Tie strings on the hanger bottom. Attach objects to the strings. Hang the mobile from the hanger hook.

5- to 6-Year-Olds

- Experiment with stationary and moving objects by attaching some items with pipe cleaners, some with string.
- Create a mobile story by using related objects.

7- to 9-Year-Olds

- This activity can be a real physics lesson in balance. Attach the spiral to a high hook or to the ceiling, and let your child work on it that way, figuring out how to keep the spiral even by distributing the weight of the objects.

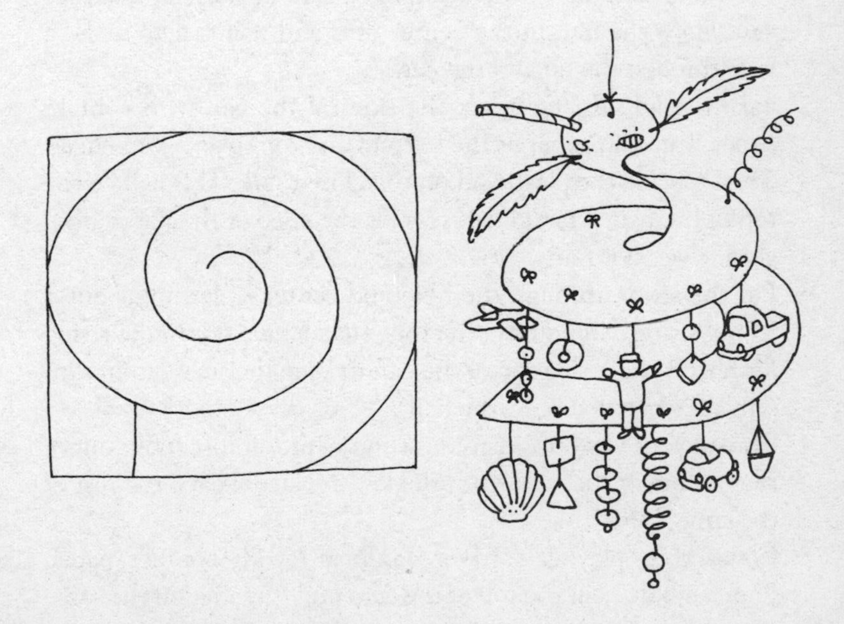

Dinner Bell

My mother always says, "Call me anything . . . except late for dinner."

MATERIALS

Metal coffee can and plastic lid
Heavy string, about 4 feet long
A large nail
A key that you don't use
Hammer
1 playing card or card-sized piece of cardboard
Colored contact paper
Scissors

DIRECTIONS

1. Put the plastic lid on the unopened side of the empty coffee can. Place the nail in the center of it and hammer to make a hole through the lid and the can.
2. Take the lid off, and cover the sides of the can with contact paper. Trim the paper at the bottom and top to get even edges. Then replace the plastic lid on the closed side. This will be the top of the bell. The lid will protect the edge of the paper from getting wet if it rains.
3. Put the string through the hole and center it, letting about 3 feet of string extend from the top. Tie a large knot in the string flush with the inside top of the can to keep the string from slipping off when you hang the bell.
4. Thread your key on the inside string so that it just sticks out of the bottom of the can. Knot the key in place. Leave the rest of the string long.
5. Cover your playing card or cardboard with contact paper. Punch a hole near the top of the card and thread it on the same

string as the key. This will be your handle. Knot the card in place about 2 or 3 inches from the bottom of the key. Cut the remaining string.

6. Hang your bell where everyone's sure to hear it.

VARIATIONS

3- to 4-Year-Olds

- Decorate the can with stickers instead of contact paper.
- Use jingle bells instead of a key for the chime.

5- to 6-Year-Olds

- Find other materials that will chime.

7- to 9-Year-Olds

- Make a melodious mobile using three different sizes of cans hung from the same string.

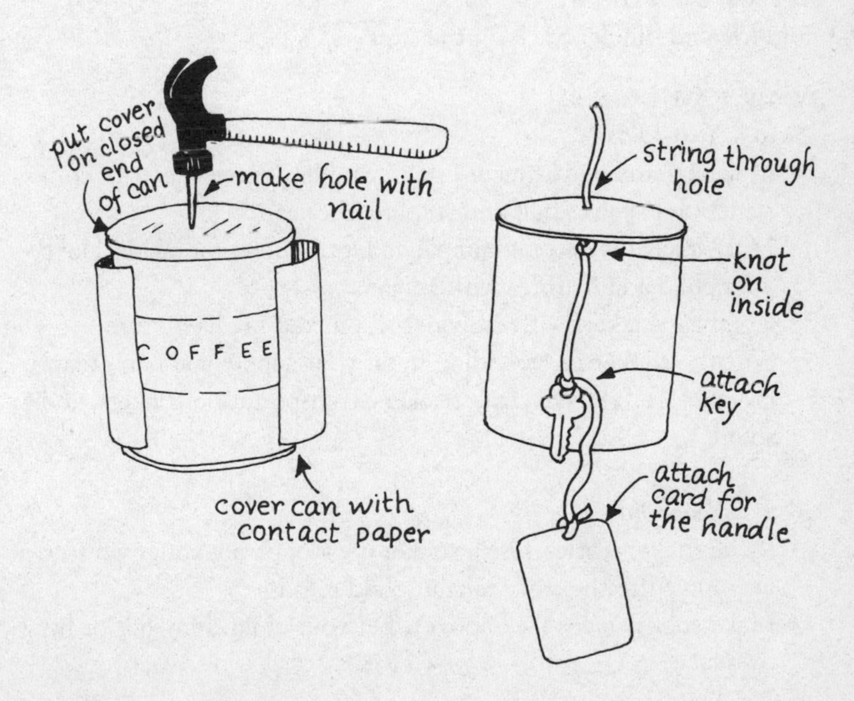

Stickers

Stickers are the Colorforms of the '90s. I keep a generous supply on hand at all times.

MATERIALS

Stickers: Use themed ones, such as animals, boats, trains, or flowers; fancy ones, such as oilies, smellies, fuzzies, or glow-in-the-dark ones; and plain stationery-store ones, such as colored circles, triangles, or squares.
Something to stick them on: Some good examples are plastic storage boxes (any size), cardboard shoe boxes, plastic picture frames, 4" x 6", unlined index cards, paper books, and sticker books.
Crayons

DIRECTIONS

1. Pure and simple: Stick on the stickers.

VARIATIONS

3- to 4-Year-Olds

- Make a permanent sticker book by folding three sheets of construction paper in half and stapling the seam.
- Make sticker faces on plain paper. Draw circles for heads. Have your child add features with stickers.
- Combine stickers with crayons for a mixed-media picture.
- Sort the stickers: Depending upon your supply you can create groups of red stickers, fruit stickers, transportation stickers, and so on.

5- to 6-Year-Olds

- Make sticker stories. Use a sticker book or create your own (see above). Write the story as your child tells it.
- Make sticker faces (see above). Let your child draw her or his own face.

- Make stationery with 4" x 6" index cards.
- Sort the stickers. Depending upon the supply, the children can create groups of little things, big things, things they'd see at school, things that grow, and the like.

7- to 9-Year-Olds

- Trading is big business at this age.
- Instead of sorting, children will probably prefer to organize their sticker books according to their own systems.
- Picture frames and boxes also appeal to this child's sense of order.
- Postcards and stationery are fun and useful.
- Homework folders can be personalized with stickers.

HINTS

- You'll be surprised how happy kids will be doing this on plain paper. However, sticker books have special paper that allows children to remove and reuse the stickers.
- Small plastic boxes or picture frames are ideal media for stickers and make great gifts.
- Large plastic boxes and shoe boxes are also good and make nice storage chests for crayons or collections.
- For instant postcards, use one side of a 4" x 6" unlined index card.
- Fold index cards to create informal note paper.

Collectors' Boxes

These boxes are collectors' items, in every sense of the word.

MATERIALS

A shoe box and cover
A variety of colored tissue paper
White glue
Small bowl or pie dish for glue
Paintbrush
Scissors

DIRECTIONS

1. Pour some glue into the small bowl or pie dish. Dilute it by about a third with water.
2. Cut or tear tissue paper into small, free-form pieces.
3. Starting with one side, "paint" the shoe box with white glue. Take scraps of paper from the glue bowl and press them on the side, covering the entire surface.
4. Repeat the process on all sides and on the box top until the whole box is covered with paper and color.
5. Trim or glue down any loose flaps.
6. Brush glue over the entire box to give it a shine. Let it dry for at least an hour.

VARIATIONS

3- to 4-Year-Olds

- Tag the finished box, using a stick-on file label designating "Crayons" or "Little People" or "Cars."

5- to 6-Year-Olds

- Glue sequins or buttons on the box after the children have finished with the paper.
- Use wrapping-paper scraps instead of tissue paper. This is especially good to do after a birthday party!

7- to 9-Year-Olds

- Attach the lid to the box to make a flip top. Cut the two corner seams on one long side of the box top so that the lip of the box top can act as a hinge. Use a hole-puncher or scissors to make two holes in the "hinge." Make two matching holes on the box side. Connect the top to the bottom with paper fasteners.

Grrreat Animal Masks

It's a jungle out there . . . so join the fun.

MATERIALS

Dinner-sized paper plates (cardboard, not Styrofoam)
A piece of elastic thread approximately ¼" wide and 8" long for each mask
A variety of colored construction paper
Ribbons or yarn for hair
Feathers
Pipe cleaners
Markers
Scissors
Stapler
Glue

DIRECTIONS

1. Hold the plate up to your child's face and make dots approximately where the eyes, nose, and mouth are.
2. Cut out holes for the eyes and mouth. If you want to make a symmetrical hole, gently fold the plate and cut on the fold.
3. Cut a breathing flap for the nose by making a long horizontal cut over the mouth area. Wider is better, as the nose flap will probably be an important feature of the mask. Then cut vertical slits going upward off each end of the horizontal line. You should now have a flap. Fold it at the top (uncut) edge so it sticks up slightly. Don't cut it off!
4. Cut a piece of elastic thread to fit three-quarters of the way around your child's head. Staple one side to the plate. Hold the plate up to the child's face, size the elastic, and staple the other side so it's secure. (Using wider, ¼" thread instead of traditional skinny thread makes the mask stronger, and better able to support all the collage materials to come.)

5. Decorate the mask! Using markers, cut-up colored paper, glue, and accessories, make your animal's face.
6. Add pipe cleaner or feather whiskers, a mane of yarn or ribbon, and a long paper nose or beak. Don't forget the ears!
7. Let the mask dry . . . and try it on.

VARIATIONS

3- to 4-Year-Olds

- Make imaginary animals and give them names, for instance, a "girelephant" has an elephant's trunk and a giraffe's spots.

5- to 6-Year-Olds

- Make more elaborate collages using glitter glue, sequins, and buttons.
- Make up stories about the animals.

7- to 9-Year-Olds

- Make handheld masks instead of face masks by attaching the plate to a wooden dowel or decorated paper towel tube.
- Make half-face masks by cutting the plate above the mouth area and elaborately decorating the eyes.

HINT

- This activity is a terrific Halloween project. Your masks don't have to be animals. They can be anything you want!

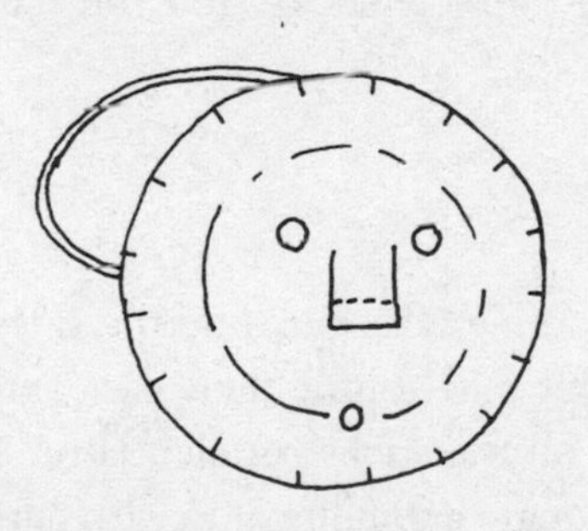

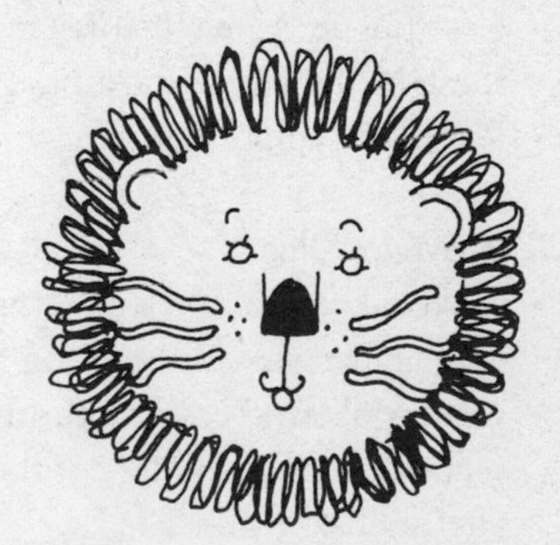

Pop Sculptures

Imaginations soar . . . and the sky is, literally, the limit.

MATERIALS

Popsicle sticks: You can buy these by the bag. Or else eat a lot of ice cream!

White glue

DIRECTIONS

1. Take a stick. Put glue on the edges.
2. Stick it to another stick.
3. Repeat. And repeat. And repeat.

VARIATIONS

3- to 4-Year-Olds

- Make a base for the sticks with a piece of cardboard. The kids can start building by putting the glue on the base and working up. If they're making a popsicle stick box, the base will serve as the bottom.
- Use tongue depressors instead of popsicle sticks. You can buy these by the box at most pharmacies.
- Paint the sculpture after it dries.

5- to 6-Year-Olds

- Make a box. Form a square with four sticks. Build up the sides log-cabin style—alternating north and south, then east and west. Make the base by running all the sticks parallel. Form a separate top by making another square and filling it in with parallel sticks.

- Make a picture frame. Form a square with four sticks. Make the sides a little thicker with a few more layers. When it's dry, tape a picture to the back.
- Make a skyscraper. See how high it can go.

7- to 9-Year-Olds

- Make a box that's not square. Try a parallelogram (a rectangle with slanted sides), a triangle, or a rectangle.
- Make a sculpture to hang on the wall. This can take any form you want. When it's dry, hang it with a picture hook.
- Use toothpicks instead of popsicle sticks. Flat toothpicks work best because they hold the glue. This is a much more delicate process than the one using popsicle sticks and requires patience as well as skill.

Designer T-Shirts

What starts as an undershirt turns into a wonder-shirt! I've even done this activity for my kids' parties.

MATERIALS

Plain white cotton T-shirts
Heavy paper bags, 1 or 2 for each shirt
Masking tape
Waterproof color markers
Newspaper

DIRECTIONS

1. Wash and dry the T-shirt.
2. Lay the shirt flat and put a paper bag inside the body. This will keep the markers from going through both sides of the cotton. You should also put paper inside the sleeves, so as not to limit creative space.
3. Tape the shirt to a table or to the floor, stretching it to get out most wrinkles.
4. Very important! Put newspaper around the shirt to keep marker scribbles from staining anything but the shirt.
5. Lay out the markers—and draw!
6. Let the shirt dry completely before wearing.

VARIATIONS

3- to 4-Year-Olds

- Write your child's first name in bold, block letters on the shirt. Then let your child decorate the letters.
- Make details that your child can fill in, such as a pocket (What would you put in it?), a necklace (What color beads would you like to wear?), or a belt (What color?).

5- to 6-Year-Olds

- Have your child write his or her initials in lots of colors.
- Draw a scene.
- Make the alphabet or numbers.

7- to 9-Year-Olds

- Decorate tank tops or camisole-type undershirts instead of basic T's. Expect to see a fashion statement!
- Further personalize shirts by cutting—lowering the neckline, shaping the sleeves, or fringing the ends. Add beads to the fringe. Tie knots to keep the beads on.

HINT

- I find boys' and men's white undershirts—the kind that come in three-packs at a discount store—work best, but any light, solid-color T-shirt in your drawer will do. Use a size larger than usual, as the shirt's going to take a lot of washing and will be worn for a long time!

Collages

There are as many different kinds of collages as there are kids. Anything from acorns to zippers can be glued onto paper and made into a masterpiece.

MATERIALS

Paper: construction paper, craft paper, cardboard, or even paper plates. Just make sure it's sturdy enough to hold the glued-on materials.

Collage materials: Try torn-up paper, feathers, buttons, ribbons, fabric, newspapers, tissue paper, wrapping paper, aluminum foil, toilet paper tubes, sequins, string.

Squeeze-bottles of white glue

DIRECTIONS

1. Spread out your base paper.
2. Choose your collage materials.
3. Glue them on!

VARIATIONS

3- to 4-Year-Olds

- Create a "playground." Fold paper for steps; use tubes for slides and tunnels. Paint the collage when you're done.

5- to 6-Year-Olds

- Choose a color theme for the collage: Glue on everything red, or blue, for example.

- Make a beach scene, using actual sand and shells. Or a garden, using flowers.
- Make a collage using circles only—Lifesavers candy, rings, washers.
- Try a collage with squares or rectangles.

7- to 9-Year-Olds

- Set up a still life; then copy it in collage materials. For example, if it's a bowl of fruit, find yellow paper to make the bananas, red foil for the cherries, a pipe cleaner for the grape stems.
- Create a collage portrait of a real or an imaginary person.

HINTS

- I keep a huge collage box filled with materials we can always use. All year long, I collect materials—torn wrapping paper, holiday ribbons, broken bead necklaces, foil, doilies, and the like.
- We also have collage walks on which we gather outside materials such as leaves, nuts, stones, or twigs to make a picture.

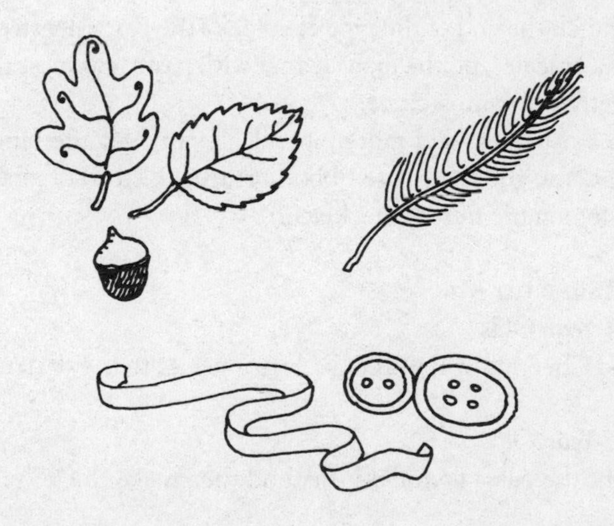

Totally Tubular Jewelry

Totally awesome!

MATERIALS

Colored pipe cleaners

Tubular pasta: ziti, penne, even wagon wheels . . . as long as there's a hole to thread through

Ribbon or string (optional)

DIRECTIONS

1. Thread the pasta on pipe cleaners to make different kinds of jewelry. Start with one pipe cleaner and one piece of pasta. Scrunch the end of the pipe cleaner so the pasta doesn't fall off.
2. For a bracelet, fill the pipe cleaner with pasta and twist the ends together to form a circle.
3. For a necklace, add more pipe cleaners to get the length you want. You could also use ribbon or string instead of pipe cleaners for a more flexible necklace.

VARIATIONS

3- to 4-Year-Olds

- Add Cheerios or Fruit Loops cereal pieces to the designs.

5- to 6-Year-Olds

- Paint the pasta first. Let it dry and then make the jewelry.

7- to 9-Year-Olds

- Make charm bracelets. Twist two or three colored pipe cleaners together into a bracelet. Tie on individual pasta "charms."
- Make a necklace by stringing pasta on a ribbon and adding hanging "charms" at the bottom.

HINTS

- Make necklaces using red licorice strings instead of pipe cleaners or ribbon. Have "beads" of Lifesavers candy and Cheerios and Fruit Loops cereal pieces. The jewelry may not last as long, but it's a lot of fun to make—and eat!
- Dye the pasta first by putting dry pasta in a plastic bag with a few drops of food coloring. Shake the bag till the pasta is colored. Let it dry. You can also color the pasta using silver or gold spray paint. Spread the pasta on a newspaper. Spray it. Let it dry. Turn it over and spray the other side.

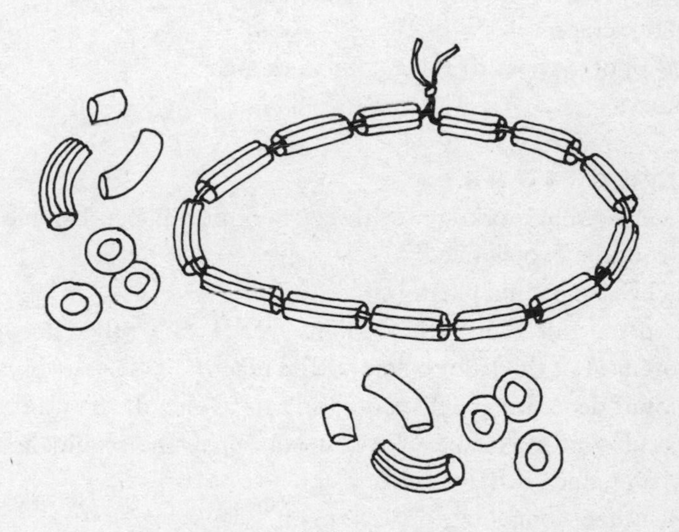

The Mad Hatter

This project is really messy, but the end result is so spectacular, it's worth all the glitter you'll be cleaning up for the next week!

MATERIALS

A plain hat for each child: Simple baseball hats are ideal, but painters' caps or even plastic sun visors will do too.

Fabric paint: You can buy this in any art supply store. It's special paint that comes in a squeeze bottle and is made especially to stick onto fabric. It comes in lots of colors and variations—puffy paint, glitter paint, translucent shinies, and neons are some types. Buy at least four colors or types.

Glitter

Sequins

Fake jewels, beads, and buttons

Fabric scraps

Lots of newspaper to cover your work area

Smocks

DIRECTIONS

1. Cover your work area with layers of newspaper. Double what you think you'll need!
2. Give each child a hat.
3. Spread out the glitter, sequins, beads, and other decorating items. Put the paint colors within reach.
4. Start decorating! The paint also acts as glue. If you want to use sequins, for example, dot paint on, press the sequins into the paint, and let them dry.
5. Let hats completely dry overnight.

VARIATIONS

3- to 4-Year-Olds

- Simplify the process by squiggling paint all over the hat and letting your child decorate with glitter, sequins, and beads.
- Write your child's name or initials in choice colors and let the child add the glitz.

5- to 6-Year-Olds

- Name-writing is fun, as is drawing flowers, rainbows, and shapes.

7- to 9-Year-Olds

- "Less is more" does not apply to this age. More paint, more decorations, more time to dry is the general idea.
- Create themes: school colors, American flag, flowers, etc.

HINTS

- The day before you do this project, test the fabric paints on a plain piece of cloth. The colors you see in the tubes may be hard to imagine dry, especially puffy formulas and translucents. Seeing how the colors dry can help your child in creating a design.
- Even though my kids adore it, glitter is not my favorite thing. If you feel the same way, buy glitter fabric paint. You'll get the same effect of glitz without all the mess.

Personal Place Mats

Even vegetables taste good when you have a personal place mat.

MATERIALS

A roll of clear contact paper
Large sheets of 12" x 18" colored construction paper
Photos of your child
Collage materials such as feathers, glitter, sequins, and tissue paper
Scissors

DIRECTIONS

1. Have the children pick out pictures of themselves, friends, and family for their mats.
2. Lay a large sheet of construction paper on the table for each child.
3. Arrange the pictures on the paper mats.
4. Design the rest of each mat by arranging collage materials around the pictures.
5. Cut two sheets of contact paper, slightly larger than 12" x 18", for each mat. Remove the protective backing from the first sheet and place the sheet over the entire construction paper design. Smooth out the bubbles.
6. Turn the place mat over and cover the back with the other sheet of contact paper. Smooth it. Now the place mat is sealed and can be cleaned with a sponge after using.
7. Trim the edge of the contact paper to even the sides.

VARIATIONS

3- to 4-Year-Olds

- Use stickers on construction paper instead of photos.
- Write the child's name on the paper before sealing.

5- to 6-Year-Olds

- "Frame" the photos by cutting shapes out of a second sheet of construction paper and placing it on top of the first. Sandwich the pictures between the two, letting them show through the shapes.
- Instead of using photos, create a woven placemat. Cut two pieces (at least) of construction paper into 1" wide strips. Cut one sheet vertically and one horizontally to get different lengths. Weave a pattern of strips on top of the flat piece of paper. Fold another piece of construction paper in half and cut out a large shape (heart, triangle, circle, or even free-form). Unfold, and place the paper on top of the pattern. The weaving will show through in whatever shape has been created. Smooth contact paper on both sides of the mat to seal and trim edges.

7- to 9-Year-Olds

- Create theme place mats by cutting pictures from magazines and using them instead of photos.
- Create friends place mats by using pictures of the kids' pals.
- Create clear collage place mats by working directly on one sheet of contact paper. Use glitter, sequins, and papers. Then carefully place the second sheet of contact paper on top to seal. Trim the edges to even.

Playful Dough

Do they ever outgrow play dough? I don't think so. Thank goodness for this homemade recipe. It's not as crumbly as the store-bought stuff, and it lasts for months in a plastic bag in the refrigerator. I always have several colors on hand.

MATERIALS

2 cups flour
1 cup salt
1 tablespoon cream of tartar
2 cups water
Food coloring
2 tablespoons vegetable oil
Pot for mixing
Wooden spoon
Measuring cup

DIRECTIONS

1. Mix the flour, salt, and cream of tartar in the pot.
2. Measure the water and add food coloring. Use one color or mix your own. Make it intense, with at least five drops of color.
3. Add the colored water and oil to the pot of dry ingredients.
4. Cook over low heat, stirring constantly. The mixture will gradually thicken. Don't worry if it's lumpy. Keep cooking about 5 minutes until it seems to form a ball.
5. Take the dough out of the pot and knead it.
6. Let the dough cool. Play!

VARIATIONS

3- to 4-Year-Olds

- Get out your cookie cutters and make shapes.
- Use popsicle sticks to "cut" the dough.

5- to 6-Year-Olds

- Roll out your dough with a rolling pin. Find things for making patterns on it: a fork; the wheels of a small truck; fingers, and other textured items.

7- to 9-Year-Olds

- Use the dough like clay to make sculptures. Squish them and start again.
- Use different colors to create designs, a map, a face.

HINT

- Divide the recipe in half and make two different colors.

Outdoor Art Projects

The beauty of the great outdoors is that you can make a fabulous mess—and just hose it off. Sand and dirt, sticks and stones, chalk, water, and leaves—all the things kids love to play with are right under their feet.

Soap Paint

The epitome of good, clean fun!

MATERIALS

Powdered Ivory soap
Water
Food coloring
Bowls for paint
Spoons for stirring
Paint brushes
Finger-painting paper

DIRECTIONS

1. Make "paint" by pouring soap flakes into a large bowl and adding water. Start with 4 cups of soap and 2 cups of water. Stir till smooth. Add more water, a little at a time, if the mixture seems too thick.
2. Divide the paint into smaller bowls, and stir a few drops of food coloring into each.
3. Let the paint set for about 10 minutes.
4. Paint! You can make big blobs, smooth, soapy smushes, or regular colored strokes.
5. Let the picture dry completely. Wash your hands and brushes in warm water and make a sinkful of bubbles!

VARIATIONS

3- to 4-Year-Olds

- Pour about an inch of soap into greased cupcake molds. Let it harden. Remove the individual cakes of soap.
- Use wide painters' brushes to paint your patio or driveway. Hose it off!

5- to 6-Year-Olds

- Don't add food coloring. Paint your outdoor furniture or bikes. After painting, take a scrub brush and really clean. Hose off everything!

7- to 9-Year-Olds

- Make some of the paint really thick and build a soap sculpture.

Nature Rubbings

This activity is a fun way to observe nature and spark imaginations. It's amazing what you've never noticed before.

MATERIALS

White paper: Computer paper, newsprint, and construction paper all work great.

Crayons

A variety of leaves, tree bark, and outside surfaces to rub

DIRECTIONS

1. Start with one leaf. Place it on a flat surface. Put the paper on top of it. Rub a crayon over the paper. The leaf outline and veins will show up.
2. Find other things to rub. To do a tree, place the paper directly on the tree and color the paper until the bark outline comes through.

VARIATIONS

3- to 4-Year-Olds

- Rub several leaves on the same paper using different color crayons.

5- to 6-Year-Olds

- See how many different leaves you can find to rub.
- Try rubbing pinecones or evergreen branches.
- Cut out the rubbings and glue them on a collage.

7- to 9-Year-Olds

- Rub a leaf, some bark, and a nut from the same tree.
- Identify the tree.
- Rub something with raised letters or numbers on it, such as a house number or a bike logo.
- Rub sidewalk cracks and wood decking.
- Rub fabric, such as burlap or denim.

Stone Age Sculptures

Create a stone zoo . . . or troll . . . or fire truck . . . or anything else. There's nothing prehistoric about these sculptures, and they're great for any age!

MATERIALS

A collection of stones and rocks
White glue
Markers

DIRECTIONS

1. Gather your stones.
2. Lay them out and see if any of the larger ones resemble a figure. If not, use your imagination to create one.
3. Glue the stones together to make a body with feet and a head, or make a car with four wheels, or an animal such as a bird.
4. Let the glue dry. With your markers, draw on details such as eyes, car windows, or whatever else your sculpture needs.

VARIATIONS

3- to 4-Year-Olds

- Paint the sculpture using poster paints.
- Create several animals and make a zoo.

5- to 6-Year-Olds

- Add collage details such as buttons or feathers.

7- to 9-Year-Olds

- Make stone paperweights for gifts. Find interesting-looking stones and paint them with poster paint. When they're dry, cover them with clear shellac.
- Look for stones that are actually shaped like things, a footprint, for example. Paint them to resemble the real thing.

Tie-Dye Flowers

Make your own garden bouquet. It's fun to do outside, where the real flowers can inspire you.

MATERIALS

Bowls of water
Food coloring
Cone-shaped coffee filters
Lots of rubber bands (Smaller is better.)
Pipe cleaners
Tongs for dipping
Newspaper for drying

DIRECTIONS

1. Fill each bowl with water and a few drops of food coloring. Mix colors to create new ones (blue and red make purple, for example).
2. Take a coffee filter and fold it lengthwise two or three times. Then wrap it with rubber bands.
3. Holding the filter with the tongs, dip it in one bowl. Keep dipping till it's saturated with colored water. Then lay it (still wrapped) on the newspaper to drip dry.
4. Repeat the process with another filter and another color.
5. When the dipped filters have dried for a few minutes, you can unwrap the rubber bands and spread the filters flat until they're completely dry.
6. Take three dried, colored filters and place them one inside the other. Push a pipe cleaner through the pointed ends, letting about an inch come through the filters. The long end will become the stem. Secure the stem by twisting the paper around the pipe cleaner and wrapping it with a clean rubber band. Spread open the filter "petals" and bend the stem.

VARIATIONS

3- to 4-Year-Olds

- Fill a clear, plastic water bottle with a little sand or some rocks to weight it down. Put the flowers in it for a vase.

5- to 6-Year-Olds

- Cut the edges of the filters with pinking shears to make tulips. Round the edges for roses. See what other kinds of flowers you can make.

7- to 9-Year-Olds

- Tie-dye a handkerchief to make a cool bandana. Mix colors by dipping the handkerchief once, adding more rubber bands, then dipping the handkerchief in a second dye.

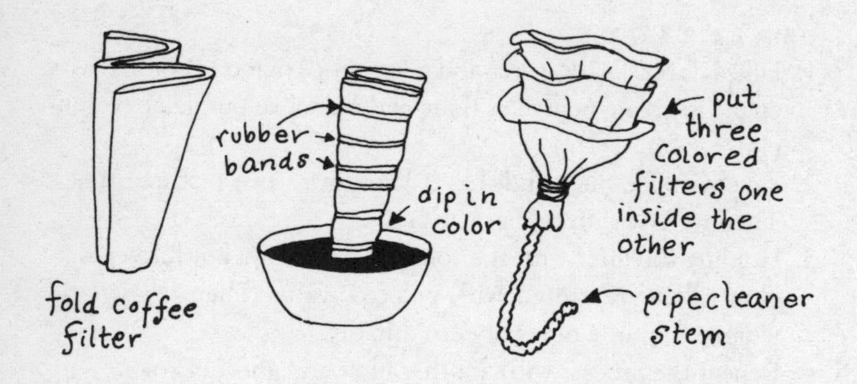

Papier-Mâché Masks

Papier-mâché can be made anytime and any place. The reason I've included it as an outside activity is that it's so messy. I think anything that can be cleaned up with a hose belongs outside.

MATERIALS

Flour
Water
Lots of newspaper, cut into long, inch-wide strips
Bowl for mixing
A bowl for each child to use as a mask mold
Waxed paper
Poster paints and brushes
Collage materials: feathers, yarn, sparkles, beads, and so on
White glue

DIRECTIONS

1. Mix a paste of flour and water in the bowl. It should have the consistency of slushy ice cream . . . not too thick, not too thin. Make a lot!
2. Invert your "mold" bowl. This is what you'll use to make your mask shape. Place a sheet of waxed paper over the bowl. This will keep the mask from sticking to the bowl. Fold the paper inside the rim, so it stays in place.
3. Dip a strip of newspaper into the paste. Drape the strip across your mold bowl. Continue doing this until the entire surface of the bowl (and the waxed paper) is covered. For good measure, add one more layer.
4. Let the papier-mâché dry overnight. It might even take two nights. Once the newspaper mask is dry, remove the bowl and, if possible, the waxed paper.
5. You should now have a round, half-bowl mask. Trim the edges

to make it smooth. Paint on a face. Add collage feathers, sparkles, or yarn hair with glue. Hang it on the wall.

VARIATIONS

3- to 4-Year-Olds

- Help your child make a self-portrait. Paint the eyes his or her color. Make yarn hair just like his or her own. Add on details such as freckles or dimples.

5- to 6-Year-Olds

- Cut out the eyes and the mouth. Make two small nose holes. Attach two ribbons on the sides and tie them so your child can wear the mask.
- Make a monster mask. Or a wild animal.

7- to 9-Year-Olds

- Add texture in the papier-mâché . . . make raised eyebrows or a nose. Make an elephant's trunk or dog ears.

Herb Pots

This activity is a great way to get kids to try new foods. Herbs usually grow quickly and easily.

MATERIALS

Small flowerpots filled with potting soil
Herb seeds, or seedlings from a nursery
Water
Waterproof markers

DIRECTIONS

1. Determine what herb (or herbs) your children will grow. Help them pick something you think they'll like to eat. Some good choices are dill, mint, basil, and parsley.
2. Have the children plant the seeds or seedlings in their flowerpots. Water the pots and place them on a sunny windowsill.
3. With the waterproof marker, write the herb name on the pot.
4. Water as needed. When the plants are grown, snip herbs off and use them.

VARIATIONS

3- to 4-Year-Olds

- Plan what foods to eat with the herbs.

5- to 6-Year-Olds

- Decorate the herb pot with colored markers. Try to draw the herb on it.

7- to 9-Year-Olds

- Look up recipes that use herbs. Think of mint tea, pesto sauce, dill sauce, and herb butters.
- Taste the fresh herb and then taste the same dried herb from the spice rack. Compare the flavors.

Creative Cachepots

This project is one of those that take several stages to complete. Start it outdoors, where the messy papier-mâché part can be cleaned with a hose. Decorate another day, indoors or out. Have patience . . . the result is worth the wait!

MATERIALS

Quart or pint milk cartons
Newspaper, cut into long, inch-wide strips
Flour
Water
Mixing bowl
Cut-up tissue paper
White glue
Another bowl
Wide paint brush

DIRECTIONS

1. The first day, make the papier-mâché pot. Mix the papier-mâché paste by combining the flour and water in a bowl until the paste is the consistency of slushy ice cream.
2. Cut the milk carton horizontally about 4 inches from the bottom. This will be your pot. If you have very small flowerpots to put in the cachepot, cut only 3 inches from the bottom. If you use a half-gallon carton, cut about 6 inches from the bottom.
3. Dip the newspaper strips in the papier-mâché paste, and wrap them on the outside of the milk carton pot. Wrap all around the sides and bottom, but not the inside. You want to keep the inside clean because that's where you'll be watering your plant.
4. Once the carton is completely and generously covered, turn it upside down to dry. This may take a day or two.
5. After your pot is dry, decorate it with tissue paper decoupage.

Fill a bowl with white glue. Dilute the glue by about a third with water. Paint the glue all over one side of your pot. Stick pieces of tissue paper on the glued side. Then paint glue over the paper to give it a shiny finish.

6. Decoupage all four sides, and the bottom if you wish. Finish the entire surface with one more coating of glue. Turn it upside down to dry.
7. When the cachepot is completely dry, use it to hold a flowerpot and place it in the center of your picnic table!

VARIATIONS

3- to 4-Year-Olds

- Paint the cachepot instead of using decoupage.
- Try decoupage with colored glue. (Elmer's glue comes in neon colors.)

5- to 6-Year-Olds

- Plant tissue paper flowers in the pot. Cut circles of tissue paper. Twist two or three into cone shapes, and add a pipe cleaner stem. Anchor them in the cachepot with rocks.
- Make Tie-Dye Flowers and plant them in your cachepot. (See page 117.)

7- to 9-Year-Olds

- Cut up magazines to use instead of tissue paper for more intricate decoupage designs. Make sure to cover the entire surface with glue.

Mud and Plaster

A winning combination for kids who like to get messy.

MATERIALS

Plaster of paris
Mixing bowl or pail
Water
Shovel
A place with loose soil or sand to dig in

DIRECTIONS

1. Dig a wide, shallow hole in the ground . . . or in your backyard sandbox.
2. Make a shape in the hole. For example, use your finger to write your initial, draw a face, or make a simple picture. Make geometric shapes, using the flat side of a shovel, or just dig a free-form hole.
3. Mix the plaster according to directions on the box. It should be liquid, but not runny. Pour or shovel it into the hole. Smooth the top. Wait for the plaster to dry. It may be an hour or two.
4. When the plaster is dry, dig around it to remove it. Brush or rinse off the dirt—and you have a perfect plaster cast!

VARIATIONS

3- to 4-Year-Olds

- After digging the hole, press a sand mold in it to create a shape. The sand mold should be upside down, so the image is concave.

The outside impression of the sand mold will become the inside impression in the hole. Remove the mold before pouring in plaster. The plaster cast will look like your sand mold.

- You can also make casts by pouring plaster directly into the sand molds. If you put a thin layer of sand on the mold first, the plaster will come out more easily, and an interesting texture will be created on your cast.

5- to 6-Year-Olds

- Before pouring the plaster, have your child decorate his or her design by adding sticks or small stones or even feathers to the hole.

7- to 9-Year-Olds

- Paint the finished plaster casts with acrylics or poster paints.

Sunny Day Sundial

One of the oldest and most fun ways to tell time.

MATERIALS

12" x 12" piece of plywood
An empty spool
A pencil or thin dowel
Ruler
Thumbtacks
Wood glue
Waterproof marker

DIRECTIONS

1. Glue the spool to the center of the plywood base. Put the dowel inside the spool. Draw a large circle around the entire base.
2. Place the plywood on a level surface, outdoors, where it will get plenty of sunlight.
3. Beginning at 12 noon, note where your pencil shadow is cast and mark the spot on the base circle with a thumbtack. Write in the time with the marker.
4. Every hour until the sun goes down, put in another tack and write the time. In the morning, start again and note from 7 to 11 A.M.

VARIATIONS

3- to 4-Year-Olds

- How many clocks can your child find in your house?
- How many different types of clocks can he or she find?

5- to 6-Year-Olds

- How many kinds of timepieces can your child read? Try: traditional clock with Arabic numerals, digital clock, sundial, clock with Roman numerals.

7- to 9-Year-Olds

- Make a more sophisticated sundial by figuring out the latitude in which you live. Start with the same 12" x 12" plywood base. Cut a "gnomon" out of another piece of plywood. The gnomon is a right angle triangle in which the southern angle equals your hometown latitude. Position the right angle of the gnomon in the center of the base and glue it in place. At 12 noon (1 P.M. DST), turn the dial so the gnomon casts the narrowest shadow possible. Mark that spot on the dial with a thumbtack or marker. As above, note the new shadow position at every hour.

HINT

- Your sundial will lose its accuracy after a few days because the angle of the sun's rays shifts with the seasons. Watch what happens after a month—and then after two months.

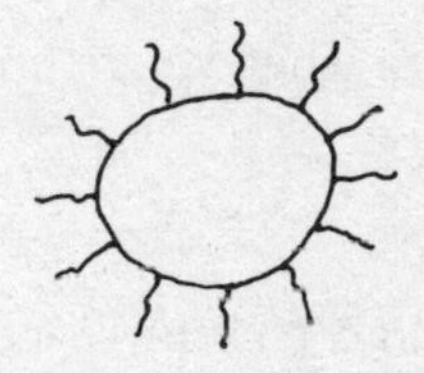

A-mazing Chalk Drawings

You call that a driveway? I call it a giant blackboard!

MATERIALS

A driveway, sidewalk, or patio on which to draw
Colored sidewalk chalk (the thick, powdery kind of chalk)
Hose or pail with water for cleaning up

DIRECTIONS

1. Define your drawing area. The bigger the better.
2. Draw a maze. Start in the center area and draw yourself "out." To make a path, use chalk in two hands and walk as you draw. Otherwise, use two children walking and drawing together.
3. Once you've completed your maze, go back inside and decorate it with drawings.
4. Hose away your work when you're finished.

VARIATIONS

3- to 4-Year-Olds

- Instead of a maze, draw parking spaces for bikes. Have the kids ride around and then park in place.
- Draw a playhouse.
- Draw place mats for a picnic lunch.

5- to 6-Year-Olds

- Pretend the maze is a neighborhood, and draw houses and stores. Use toy cars on the "street."
- Set the table for lunch by drawing silverware and plates.
- Try to walk on the maze line without falling off. Try hopping!

7- to 9-Year-Olds

- Make the maze more complex with false passageways and tricky "This Way Out" signs.

Meet Gunther Greengrass

A welcome addition to your family . . . small, quiet, and doesn't need his own room.

MATERIALS

Paper cups
Dirt
A shovel or large spoon
Grass seed
Markers or crayons
Water

DIRECTIONS

1. Draw a face on your paper cup. Some cups have built-in handles for "ears." Don't draw the hair!
2. Fill the cup two-thirds full with soil. Add water to make it wet, but don't make mud.
3. Generously sprinkle grass seed on top of the soil.
4. Cover the seeds with another thin layer of soil and lightly water the soil again.
5. Place the cup by a sunny window and wait for Gunther's hair to grow. Water every other day or whenever he gets dry.

VARIATIONS

3- to 4-Year-Olds

- Use stickers for the face instead of crayons or markers.

5- to 6-Year-Olds

- Make Greta Greengrass too.

7- to 9-Year-Olds

- Make a folded-paper collar for Gunther. Add a red bow tie.

Blowing Bubbles in the Wind

Everyone loves bubbles. Use different shapes and tools to see how big you can get them!

MATERIALS

1 cup liquid dishwashing detergent: Joy or Dawn dishwashing liquid works great.
8 cups water
1 cup Karo syrup
Straws
Wire hangers
A classic bubble wand
String
A large tub for bubble solution
Smaller bowls for extra bubble solution

DIRECTIONS

1. Mix the dishwashing detergent, water, and Karo syrup in the large tub. Then pour some of the mixture into the smaller bowls.
2. Using the straw, blow into one small bowl. Watch the bubbles appear.
3. Bend a wire hanger into a circle with a handle. Dip the wire circle in the solution in the large tub, and gently wave it in the air to make a large bubble.
4. Cut string into different lengths. Thread each string through two straws and tie the ends together. Using the straws as your two handles, carefully dip the string into the solution, pull it up to the air, and gently wave it to release the bubbles.

VARIATIONS

3- to 4-Year-Olds

- Use pipe cleaners to make bubble wands. Make big and little wands. Try different shapes.
- Try to build bubble snowmen by catching small bubbles together on a bubble wand.

5- to 6-Year-Olds

- Make bubbles in different shapes by bending or twisting the wire hangers.
- Use a fish or butterfly net to make bubbles.

7- to 9-Year-Olds

- Make the biggest string bubble you can. Have two or three children help hold the edges as they dip and wave.
- Use soda six-pack rings to make a multifaceted bubble wand.

HINT

- The bubble solution keeps well; it actually gets better as it gets older. Store it in a closed container.

Sand Paintings

Painting on sand is a whole new sensation. This mixed-media masterpiece is a perfect outdoor project.

MATERIALS

Sand
Strainer
Pails or bowls
Shovel
White glue
Pie tin for glue
Paint brushes
Poster paints
Water
A flat piece of wood or plywood, at least 8" x 11", for painting

DIRECTIONS

1. Strain the sand to clean it. Discard any leaves, sticks, and stones. Put the clean sand in a bowl or pail.
2. Pour the glue into a pie tin. Add a little water to dilute it. Brush the entire surface of your wood with glue.
3. Shovel sand onto the gluey wood. Shake the wood to cover the whole top with sand. Pat the sand with your hands. Let the board dry for about 15 minutes; then shake it upside down to get rid of excess sand.
4. Now paint a picture on the sand surface using the poster paints and clean brushes.

VARIATIONS

3- to 4-Year-Olds

- Use sidewalk chalk instead of paint on the sand. It feels funny when the children draw.

5- to 6-Year-Olds

- Glue on other outdoor materials to paint. Use sticks or small pinecones or shells.

7- to 9-Year-Olds

- Before putting on the glue, draw a picture on the wood with pencil. Glue only the places where you want sand. The finished piece will have some painted sand surfaces, some painted wooden ones, and maybe even some plain ones.

Walking Tall

Stilts make you feel like you're on top of the world. You are!

MATERIALS

2 empty coffee cans for each pair of stilts
12' long piece of heavy package string or cord for each stilt
Hammer
A large nail
Masking tape

DIRECTIONS

1. Use the hammer and nail to punch two holes in the sides of each coffee can. These are where you'll thread the string. Make the holes about an inch from the top (unopened end) of the cans, one on each side of the can.
2. Thread the string through both holes on one can. Tie the ends together with a knot on the bottom. When you pull the string up, the knot should be hidden inside the can. Repeat the process on the second can.
3. Have your child stand on the cans and hold the strings up to size them. The child should be able to hold the strings comfortably, with elbows bent. Give an extra inch or two; then make another knot (inside the cans) to shorten the strings to the exact length.
4. Put a few rows of masking tape at the top of the strings where your child's hands will hold. This will protect both string and hands.
5. Try them on . . . and walk tall!

VARIATIONS

3- to 4-Year-Olds

- Let your child put on a high hat to see if he or she is as tall as Mom.
- Allow your child to put on a pair of Dad's pants and pretend to be a grown man.

5- to 6-Year-Olds

- Have a race.

7- to 9-Year-Olds

- Walk on sand.
- Walk up a slope.
- Go backwards.

Twig Wreaths

Why wait for Christmas to hang out a wreath? Twig wreaths are a wonderful way to celebrate any season . . . and a wonderful welcome into your home.

MATERIALS

Long, soft branches: Bittersweet or grape vines work best.
An assortment of seasonal objects such as flowers, pinecones, acorns, leaves, and herbs
Thin wire or pipe cleaners
A ribbon for hanging

DIRECTIONS

1. Gather several branches. Strip off any leaves.
2. Bend the branch into a circle. For a small wreath, wrap the branch around and around itself in the size you want. Intertwine the branch as you wrap to keep it in place. Secure the ends with wire or a pipe cleaner. For a larger wreath, make one circle and secure the ends. Then wrap three or four more branches the same size. Do one at a time, intertwining them with the first circle as you wrap. Secure them all together with wire or pipe cleaners.
3. Weave flowers, leaves, or herbs between the branches.
4. Attach pinecones, acorns, or other stiff objects with wire or pipe cleaners.
5. Attach a ribbon at the top to hang your wreath.

VARIATIONS

3- to 4-Year-Olds

- Make several wreaths ahead of time and let children gather and attach objects.
- Paint the wreaths before adding decorations.

5- to 6-Year-Olds

- Use glitter glue to attach light objects such as leaves or dried flowers.
- Add sequins for sparkle.

7- to 9-Year-Olds

- Have a theme for your wreath, for example, herbs, leaves, daisies, or shells.
- Don't use living objects: Use plastic charms, ribbons, doilies, feathers. Glue them on.

HINT

- Make a memorable summer wreath by gluing seashells to your wreath. Add more glue and sprinkle the wreath with sand.

Sand Box Sculpties

A new way to play in the sand.

MATERIALS
A sandbox full of sand, or a beach
Corrugated cardboard
Scissors

DIRECTIONS
1. Before you start playing in the sand, make one or more corrugated cardboard "sculpties." Use a long piece of cardboard (if it's from a box, use one of the top or bottom flaps). Cut a pattern on two edges. For example, make a zigzag all across one side, and make a curved, snakelike edge on the other.
2. Take your sculptie into the sandbox, and run the cut edge across smooth sand. Look at the pattern!
3. Run the other edge across the sand. See how different the patterns are. Make a plaid.

VARIATIONS

3- to 4-Year-Olds
- Decorate a sand pail cake with a sculptie design.
- Make sculptie roads for sand toy trucks.

5- to 6-Year-Olds
- Sculpt your child's name in the sand.
- Make sculptie people.

7- to 9-Year-Olds
- Once your child sees how to do this, help plan sculpties according to the type of patterns he or she would like to make.
- Sculpt hills and valleys.

Seasonal Projects

From pumpkins to pinecones, starfish to snowmen, every season has a reason to celebrate.

WINTER

Store a Snowball

Want to have a snowball fight in July? All it takes is a little planning.

MATERIALS
Packing snow
Freezer bags

DIRECTIONS
1. Wait for a great snow. Then make a snowball . . . or two . . . or a dozen.
2. Pack them in freezer bags.
3. Pop them in the freezer and wait for summer.

VARIATIONS

3- to 4-Year-Olds
- Make three snowballs of different sizes. When you take them out, make a snowman!

5- to 6-Year-Olds
- Save icicles too.

7- to 9-Year-Olds
- Save a ball from every snowstorm. Date them in bags. See if the snows look different.

Snow Painting

The only graffiti I've ever appreciated!

MATERIALS

A snow-covered yard
Several spray bottles: Window cleaner or plant spritzer ones are best.
Water
Washable poster paint

DIRECTIONS

1. Fill sprayer bottles with water. Add a few drops of paint to each bottle to create "water colors."
2. Take the bottles outside in the snow and spray-paint a design.

VARIATIONS

3- to 4-Year-Olds

- Take pails and shovels. Make snow cakes and color them.

5- to 6-Year-Olds

- Make a huge snow rainbow. Make snow flowers under it.
- Make colored snowballs.

7- to 9-Year-Olds

- Make a snowman—or a snow woman—and add color.
- Make a target and see who can hit the red bull's-eye with a snowball.

Peanut Butter Bird Feeders

A winter staple. For you, and the birds.

MATERIALS

Pinecones, as large as you can find
String
A jar of creamy peanut butter
A bag of standard birdseed
Knife for spreading peanut butter
Large bowl
Waxed paper

DIRECTIONS

1. Tie the string around the top of the pinecone and make a loop. This is how your bird feeder will hang from the tree.
2. Generously spread peanut butter all over the pinecone. Lay the pinecone on waxed paper.
3. Pour birdseed into the bowl. Roll the peanut-butter–covered pinecone in the seeds, coating all sides.
4. Hang the finished feeder from a branch that you can see.

VARIATIONS

3- to 4-Year-Olds

- Talk about the kinds of foods birds eat.
- Make your own peanut butter and "birdseed" sandwiches: Spread peanut butter on one piece of bread, honey or jelly on another. Sprinkle cold cereal on the peanut butter half: Use Cheerios cereal, cornflakes, granola, or whatever you have at hand. Make a sandwich . . . and enjoy!

5- to 6-Year-Olds

- Think of different meals you can make for the birds: birdseed, sunflower seeds, bread bits, cereals.

7- to 9-Year-Olds

- Learn the names of the birds that are eating your meals. Do different birds like different seeds?

Santa Stockings

Everyone knows that bigger is better.

MATERIALS

One 12" x 12" piece of paper to use as a template
Two 12" x 12" pieces of felt for each stocking
White glue
Glitter glue or glitter
Hole punch
Large yarn needle
Yarn
Pencil
Scissors
Straight pins

DIRECTIONS

1. Draw a stocking shape on the template paper and cut it out.
2. Place the template on top of the two pieces of felt. Pin it in place.
3. Cut the two pieces of felt around the template. Unpin the paper.
4. Glue the two sides of the stocking together by putting a stream of white glue around the edge of one piece of felt. Don't glue the top edge! Put the other piece of felt in place and press. Let the stocking dry.
5. Using the hole punch, make holes at 1-inch intervals all around the dry stocking. Start at the top left corner and work down and around until you reach the top right corner. Don't punch the top—you need to leave it open!
6. Thread the yarn needle with the yarn, and sew in and out of the holes all the way around the stocking. Make loops at both of the corners for hanging.

7. Write your child's name on the stocking with glitter glue. If you're using glitter, write the name in white glue and sprinkle glitter on top. When it's dry, shake off the excess glitter.

VARIATIONS

3- to 4-Year-Olds

- Make glitter-glue or glitter designs on the stocking.

5- to 6-Year-Olds

- Sew two yarns of different colors through the holes for a more colorful effect.
- Use another piece of felt to make a cuff on the stocking, or cut out shapes to glue on.

7- to 9-Year-Olds

- Write the kids' names in yarn. Glue them on with glitter glue.

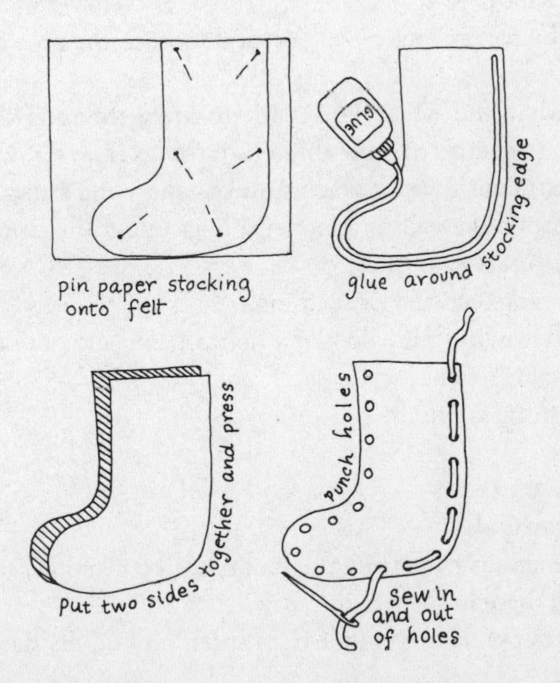

SPRING

Plant a Garden

Nothing tastes better than food you grow yourself!

MATERIALS

A plot of land
Hoe and shovel
Stakes
String
Fertilizer
Seeds and seedlings (a combination)

DIRECTIONS

1. Prep the soil in your plot. Hoe and fertilize the area for planting.
2. Plan what and where you want to grow things. Don't overcrowd. It's better to grow three lush things than ten wimps.
3. Make straight rows by placing stakes and tying string between them. Sprinkle seeds or plant seedlings under the string. Cover with a thin layer of soil.
4. Water each seed row or seedling.
5. Mark down on your calendar when you expect your vegetables to be ready to eat.
6. Harvest the bounty!

VARIATIONS

3- to 4-Year-Olds

- Make markers by putting the empty seed packets on sticks and placing them in their proper row.
- Have your child help water the garden on hot, dry days.

5- to 6-Year-Olds

- Have the children help weed the garden.
- Teach the kids to "deadhead" (pick dead blooms off the flowers).

7- to 9-Year-Olds

- Make the children be responsible for weeding and watering the garden.
- Let the kids help stake the plants as needed.
- Plant some perennials that will come up every year.

HINTS

- Choose things that your children will eat.
- Begin planting as soon as the ground is warm. In some areas, spring begins in March; in others, you'll have to wait till April or even May. Different plants also go in at different times.
- Mix plants that grow quickly (such as lettuce, peas, beans, or radishes) with those that take a longer time (melons, pumpkins, tomatoes, and strawberries).
- Plant an herb to try, such as dill, parsley, or basil.
- Add some seedlings for immediate gratification.
- Mix in flowers for color. Marigolds, snapdragons, and zinnias are good choices.

Maple Seed Noses

Wanna make someone smile? Put on a happy nose.

MATERIALS
Green maple tree seeds
Your nose

DIRECTIONS
1. Collect a handful of green maple tree seeds.
2. Open up the bulb end. The inside will be slightly gooey.
3. Stick the seed on your nose.

VARIATIONS
3- to 4-Year-Olds
- How many noses can the kids wear at once?
- Make happy noses with the curve pointing up and sad noses with the curve pointing down.

5- to 6-Year-Olds
- Make up characters with the noses.
- Take off the nose and make it into a helicopter by holding it above your head and letting go. Watch it twirl to a landing.

7- to 9-Year-Olds
- Whose nose can stay on the longest?

Love-a-Tree Book

This is a terrific way to record the seasons.

MATERIALS

About 10 sheets of plain white paper: Computer or typing paper is ideal.
Stapler
Crayons, colored pencils
A piece of clear contact paper, about 8" x 10"
Scotch tape

DIRECTIONS

1. Find a wonderful tree that you see every day. Look for one outside your window, in your yard, on your way to school. This will be the tree that you'll observe in your book.
2. Make your initial book by putting the sheets of white paper in a pile and stapling them on one side. You'll now have a bound edge. The book will become a scrapbook, and you'll record different aspects of your tree on each page, pasting and stapling in an assortment of items.
3. On the cover, draw a picture of your tree and date it.
4. Find out the name of your tree and write it on page 1. Tell what you like best about the tree.
5. Take a leaf from your tree and preserve it in clear contact paper. Tape the leaf to page 2 and date it.
6. Make a leaf etching for page 3. Take a leaf and place a piece of white paper over it. Very gently, using the side of a pencil or crayon, color the paper over the leaf. The outline of the leaf and its veins will show through.
7. For each subsequent page, pick another aspect of the tree to observe. Take a piece of bark. Imagine a tree house. Draw the tree in its setting. Write the date on each page.

VARIATIONS

3- to 4-Year-Olds

- Help your child paint a picture of the tree and put it in the book.
- Make a cover for the book with a 17" x 11" piece of construction paper. Gather leaves from the tree and glue them with a glue stick to the paper. Cover the entire sheet with a piece of clear contact paper. Fold the sheet in half and staple it onto the outside of the book.

5- to 6-Year-Olds

- Make a hard cover for the book with a file folder. Staple the white pages inside at the seams. Cut out pictures of trees from magazines and glue them onto the cover.
- Make a list of things that are made with trees.
- Include other kinds of trees or leaves in the book. Label them.

7- to 9-Year-Olds

- Keep a record for an entire season or a year. In the spring and fall, draw the tree at different intervals as it gains or loses leaves. Always date the pages.
- Use a Polaroid camera to record the tree in addition to the drawings.
- Find out as much as you can about the life of your tree.

Color Your Own Lilies

Who says you can't fool Mother Nature?

MATERIALS

Freshly picked lilies of the valley
Several small juice glasses
Water
Food coloring

DIRECTIONS

1. Fill the juice glasses with water. Color the water by putting a few drops of food coloring in each glass.
2. Place several sprigs of lilies in each glass, making sure the stems are covered with water and the flowers are standing up.
3. Within an hour, the colors will travel up the stems and into the flowers and you'll have made-to-order lilies! The colors will get deeper as the flowers soak.

VARIATIONS

3- to 4-Year-Olds

- For a quick trick, put stalks of celery in the colored water. The colors travel instantly and the kids will have a snack to munch while they wait for the lilies.

5- to 6-Year-Olds

- Mix new colors from the basic food coloring. Try purple, orange, and yellow-green.

7- to 9-Year-Olds

- See if this activity works with other flowers or leaves. Carnations are great flowers to color.

March Wind Chimes

What a delightful way to catch the March wind.

MATERIALS

A thick stick, about 8 inches long
A collection of at least 36 shells, different shapes and sizes
Fishing wire or nylon string
Thin nails or brads
A hammer

DIRECTIONS

1. Make a hole in the top of each shell by lightly tapping the brad with the hammer.
2. Cut eight lengths of string about 18 inches each. String on one shell and knot it in place about 5 inches from the top. Knot another shell onto the same string about 1 inch down from the first. Continue doing this until you have six shells on your string.
3. Lace shells on five more strings in the same manner.
4. Tie the strings onto the stick, starting about an inch in from the end, and placing them an inch apart. Securely knot them.
5. Tie the last two strings at each end of the stick and knot them together at the top for hanging.
6. Hang the chime where it will catch the breeze and remind you of the beach.

VARIATIONS

3- to 4-Year-Olds

- Add bells on several strings for a melodious variation.

5- to 6-Year-Olds

- Look for a piece of driftwood to use as a base instead of the stick.

7- to 9-Year-Olds

- Plan a shell design. Try using all clam shells (after a meal of steamers!) or mussels. Arrange scallop shells by size.

HINT

- Every summer we collect umpteen dozen shells, and I never have the heart to throw them away. I store them in shoe boxes and pull some out whenever we need new collage materials, inspiration for a diorama, shells for a project like this one, or just a nice reminder of how we spent our summer vacation.

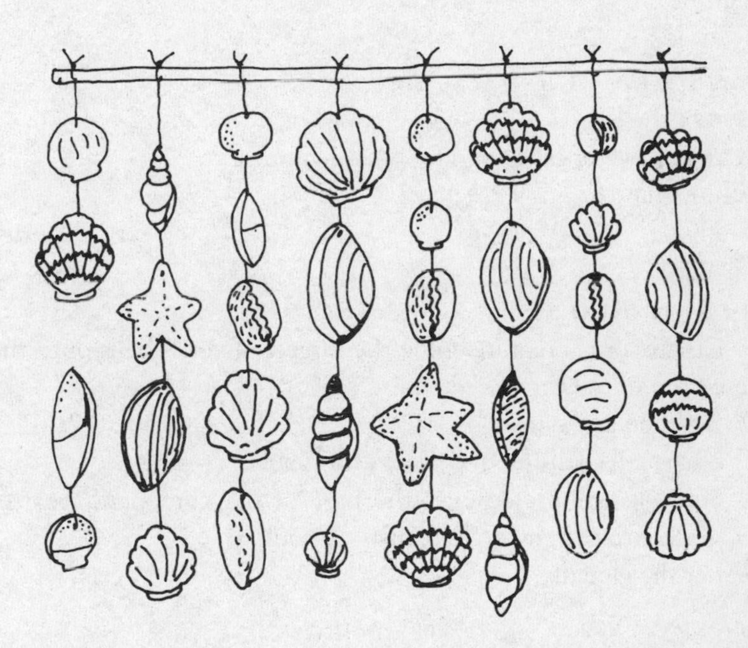

SUMMER

Creatures from the Sea

Who doesn't like to gather shells? Now here's what to do with the bounty.

MATERIALS

Lots of shells
A large piece of cardboard for each sculpture
White glue
Sand

DIRECTIONS

1. Create a sea creature. Glue the largest of your shells onto the center of the cardboard base.
2. Build up and out.
3. Use small shells for eyes, claws for hands.
4. Squiggle white glue over the base of the cardboard. Scatter sand onto the glue for a realistic "beach."
5. Let the glue dry.

VARIATIONS

3- to 4-Year-Olds

- Paint the finished sculpture with poster paints.
- Make a shell collage on construction paper.

5- to 6-Year-Olds

- Display the shells as a collection. Sort them by shape, size, or color. Draw a grid on the cardboard and glue one shell in each square.

7- to 9-Year-Olds

- Use the cover of a shoe box to create a frame for the collection. Draw a grid inside. Glue each shell into a square. Identify the shell and label it on a file label.

HINTS

- If any of your small shells have holes in them, thread them on a string and make a necklace.
- Large shells can be used as soap dishes.
- Don't forget to hold a conch shell up to your child's ear to hear the ocean!

Snow in July

This activity is one of my children's favorite "things." I've listed it as an outside project only because it can, literally, get out of hand and you'll have "snow" all over your table, floor, and clothes. The good news is . . . it's completely washable!

MATERIALS

2 cups cornstarch
1¼ cup water
Large bowl
Large spoon
Tarp or plastic tablecloth

DIRECTIONS

1. Mix cornstarch and water in the bowl. Stir till smooth. It's going to feel hard and crunchy at first, but keep stirring. You may need a touch more water.
2. Spoon the finished snow into piles on the tarp.
3. Play! The fun is in the feeling!

VARIATIONS

3- to 4-Year-Olds

- Use several paper cups and spoons to pour and scoop.
- Use a pail and shovel.

5- to 6-Year-Olds

- Put a cup of extra water nearby to refresh hard snow.
- Make snow shapes, like pancakes. Work quickly!

7- to 9-Year-Olds

- Experiment with snow as it hardens. Can you make it soft again?
- Take a garden hose and clean off the snow, the tarp, and your kids!

Flower Folders

A great way to get ready for school!

MATERIALS

Freshly picked flowers and herbs
Paper towels
A few heavy books
Colored file folders
Clear contact paper
Glue stick

DIRECTIONS

1. Pick a variety of fresh flowers and herbs. Pick them at their peak . . . before they start to wilt or brown.
2. Place the flowers flat on an absorbent paper towel. Top them with another towel.
3. Press the flowers in towels between two books. Top with several more heavy books.
4. Wait several days for the flowers to dry and flatten. This is probably the hardest part of the project! During the waiting period, take a trip to the stationer's to buy your folders. Choose colors that work with your flowers.
5. Cut contact paper to fit around the front and back of the folder, with a slight border all around.
6. Place the dried flowers on the outside front of the folder. Lightly glue them in place with the glue stick.
7. Peel the protective paper off half of the contact paper, and place the contact paper over the front, securing the flowers. Smooth out bubbles.
8. Repeat the process on the back of the folder.

9. Fold the excess contact paper inside the folder and smooth to the edges. You'll have to cut the corners of the paper to get a neat fold.

VARIATIONS

3- to 4-Year-Olds

- While this age group may not need homework folders, teacher's note folders or art folders are certainly useful.
- Have the child write his or her name on the inside.
- Tape the child's photograph to the inside.

5- to 6-Year-Olds

- Draw lines on the inside front cover and have your child write the alphabet. In three months, she or he can rewrite the alphabet on the inside back cover. Your child will be amazed at the handwriting improvement!

7- to 9-Year-Olds

- Have your child write name, address, and phone number inside the folder.
- Make a grid inside for your child to fill in with his or her fall schedule.

Water Works

On a hot day in July, create your own backyard water slide.

MATERIALS

A lawn sprinkler
A plastic tablecloth
A flat lawn area
4 stakes or heavy rocks to hold the tablecloth
Plenty of towels!

DIRECTIONS

1. Put the kids in bathing suits.
2. Spread the tablecloth on the lawn. Stake it at the corners to keep it firmly in place.
3. Aim the sprinkler so that it keeps the cloth constantly wet.
4. Have the children take a running start to the tablecloth, sit down, and sl i i i i i de.

VARIATIONS

3- to 4-Year-Olds

- Have the children run in pairs.

5- to 6-Year-Olds

- Watch the kids slide on their tummies.

7- to 9-Year-Olds

- See how far the kids can slide. Add a second cloth (and sprinkler if needed) to create a longer route.

HINT

- Make sure the stakes or rocks are not in the way of the sliders. If necessary, twist towels around the stakes to make them safe.

FALL

Pumpkin Pals

A good alternative to carved jack-o'-lanterns . . . and they last a lot longer!

MATERIALS

1 pumpkin for each child
Wide markers
Pencil
White glue
Yarn, ribbons, fabric scraps, buttons, cotton balls
Scarf or hat

DIRECTIONS

1. Plan your pumpkin face by sketching in pencil.
2. Draw the face with markers and color it in.
3. Attach details such as button eyes, a ribbon mustache, cotton eyebrows and yarn hair.
4. Add a hat or scarf.

VARIATIONS

3- to 4-Year-Olds

- Use stickers in shapes for the nose, eyes, teeth.
- Make "yourself" by putting hair and eyes in your coloring, adding your hat.

5- to 6-Year-Olds

- Make the scariest pumpkin you've ever seen.
- Make pumpkin creatures, like an octopus or a flower.

7- to 9-Year-Olds

- Use toothpicks to add on other elements such as dangling earrings, a marshmallow nose, candy corn teeth.
- Use acrylic paint for more colors and vibrancy.
- Use glow-in-the-dark paint for more fun.

Pinecone Hangings

String them across your windows for a festive fall garland.

MATERIALS

Pinecones
Poster paints
Brushes
String or thick yarn
Newspaper

DIRECTIONS

1. Gather pinecones. Brush off any leaves, grass, or dirt.
2. Paint the "branches" of the cones and lay the cones out on newspaper to dry.
3. String them for display: Lay the cones in a row, with equal spacing between them. Cut string or yarn four times the length of the row. Starting about 5 inches in from one end of the string, wrap the long end of the string evenly around the upper half of the first pinecone. Go between the branches if you can, so the cone hangs vertically. One by one, wrap each cone, leaving equal space between them. Leave about 5 inches of string on the other side.
4. Hang the garland across a window or doorway.

VARIATIONS

3- to 4-Year-Olds

- Sprinkle glitter on the pinecones while the paint is still wet.

5- to 6-Year-Olds

- Make a pinecone mobile by tying each cone individually with different lengths of string. Attach all of them to a wire hanger.

7- to 9-Year-Olds

- Make a pinecone door wreath by attaching cones to each other with pipe cleaners. Bend the pipe cleaners into a circle. Then paint. Finally, add festive decorations such as bead "berries," cotton "snow," or ribbons.

Sponge-Painted Leaves

A new take on leaf collections!

MATERIALS

A selection of fallen leaves
Construction paper
Several sponges
Pie tins, bowls, or a cupcake mold to hold paints
Poster paints
Scissors
Scotch tape or double-stick tape

DIRECTIONS

1. Lay plenty of leaves in a pattern on a sheet of construction paper. Don't cover the paper completely . . . you want to see leaf outlines.
2. Lightly tape the leaves in place by putting a circular piece of Scotch tape (or a piece of double-stick tape) on the back of each one.
3. Pour the paint into bowls.
4. Cut the sponges in half. Dip the sponges in the paints and sponge over and around the leaves.
5. When the leaves are dry, carefully remove them to reveal a wonderful leaf-patterned picture.

VARIATIONS

3- to 4-Year-Olds

- Make a collage with the painted leaves by gluing them on another piece of construction paper.

5- to 6-Year-Olds

- Press the painted leaves. Lay them between two pieces of waxed paper. Have an adult lightly iron them.

7- to 9-Year-Olds

- Make leaf rubbings by placing a thin piece of white paper (computer paper works great) over the leaf and rubbing the paper with the side of a pencil or crayon to reveal the leaf's structure.
- Use other textured items to paint with instead of sponges. Try crumbled paper towels, old toothbrushes, corduroy, even thumbs.

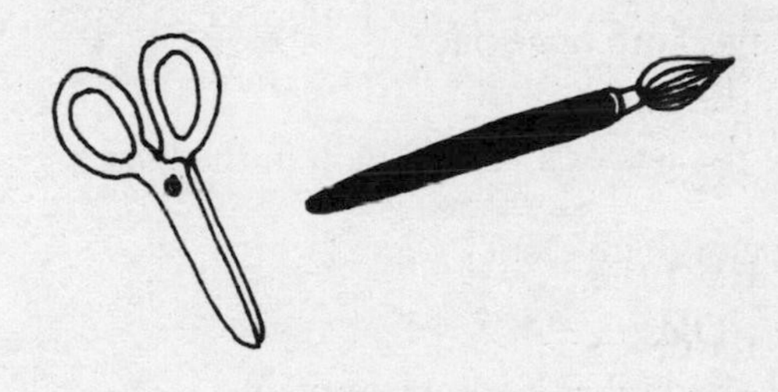

Leave it to Me

Why not have fun while cleaning up the yard?

MATERIALS

A yard full of leaves
Rakes
Leaf bags

DIRECTIONS

1. Rake leaves into huge piles
2. Jump in the piles!
3. Re-rake the leaves and put them in the bags.

VARIATIONS

3- to 4-Year-Olds

- Use kid-sized rakes if you have them.
- Make small piles as you go. Then have the kids put the small piles of leaves in a wagon and wheel them over to the "big" piles.

5- to 6-Year-Olds

- Make one huge pile. See how tall you can get it.

7- to 9-Year-Olds

- Make a mountain out of all the filled leaf bags. Watch the children climb to the top.

HINT

- Buy leaf bags printed like jack-o'-lanterns. Fill them up and get ready for Halloween!

Special Times

Cooking together, cuddling together, traveling, or teaching responsibility. Each of these areas could be a book in itself. Once again, I've chosen my family favorites, hoping they work for you too.

KIDS IN THE KITCHEN

When cooking is an activity instead of a necessity, it's a lot of fun. It's also a good way to experiment with new foods. I find that when my children help prepare a meal, they're more likely to eat it!

Yogurt Dip

The ultimate healthy treat! My kids learned to love raw vegetables this way.

INGREDIENTS

1 cup plain yogurt
Dill
Parsley
Garlic salt
Minced dry onions (optional)
Cut-up vegetables: an assortment of red peppers, green peppers, carrots, celery, snow peas, mushrooms, and other crunchy favorites

DIRECTIONS

1. Mix the spices and herbs into the yogurt. It may take some experimentation to get the right mix for your children. Start with the dill (dried or fresh). Let your children taste each spice before you add it.
2. Dip the vegetables and eat!

VARIATIONS

3- to 4-Year-Olds

- Thin carrot strips are always a good starter. Put a little dip on their plates and have children say "Dip, dip" as they try it. Once they like the dip, other vegetables will follow!
- Dip apple or pear slices in fruit yogurt.

5- to 6-Year-Olds

- Let them choose the vegetables and set them out on an hors d'oeuvres platter.
- Try making radish roses and carrot curls.

7- to 9-Year-Olds

- Try different spices and herbs to make your own dips. Curry and honey is a good combination.
- Make a classic onion dip with sour cream and dried onion soup mix.

HINTS

- Try new vegetables this way, such as raw broccoli or asparagus. Parboil some vegetable pieces and let children eat them as finger foods.
- A tablespoon of mayonnaise makes the yogurt dip a little creamier.

Scenic Salads

Food that's fun to make is *usually* fun to eat.

INGREDIENTS

Several kinds of vegetables: cherry tomatoes, lettuce, asparagus, avocado, carrots
Pasta, cooked
Grated cheese
Hard-boiled eggs
Raisins
Toothpicks
Imagination

DIRECTIONS

1. Create a picture in your mind. Assemble the ingredients and begin!

   Some suggestions: a clown with a round egg face, cherry tomato nose, raisin eyes, and pasta hair; a sailboat made from half a hard-boiled egg, with a cheddar cheese triangle sail, on a sea of lettuce; a tall man with asparagus legs, an avocado body, carrot arms, and a tomato head.
2. Admire your finished salads and dig in!

VARIATIONS

3- to 4-Year-Olds

- Help your child find a picture of something he or she likes. Together make it into a salad. Some easier suggestions: a car, a doll, a flower.

5- to 6-Year-Olds

- Make salads for each other or for the whole family.

7- to 9-Year-Olds

- Make scenes—a sunset, using strips of red pepper, carrot, and yellow pepper, and a cherry tomato; a skyscraper, made out of celery and carrots with cubed-cheese windows.

HINT

- You can also do this activity by assembling all your ingredients first, and then seeing what you can make from what's on hand.
- Some fun things to use are alfalfa sprouts, curly lettuce, sunflower seeds, and olives.

Hand Cookies

These are special-occasion cookies. They're rich and candy-coated. My kids love to make them almost as much as they love to eat them!

INGREDIENTS

For the cookies:
1 cup butter
1½ cups sugar
2 teaspoons vanilla
2 eggs
4 cups flour
1 teaspoon salt
1 teaspoon baking powder
Waxed paper
Paper
Pencil
Scissors
Rolling pin
Baking sheet
Knife
Electric mixer
For the icing:
2 cups confectioners' sugar
Water
Food coloring
or
Several tubes of ready-made decorating icings and gels
For the decorations:
Sprinkles
Chips
Decorating candies

DIRECTIONS

1. Make the cookie dough: Cream the butter, sugar, and vanilla until smooth and fluffy. Add the eggs, and continue beating till blended. Gradually blend the flour, salt, and baking powder. Wrap the dough in waxed paper and chill it for 30 minutes. While it's chilling, make your handprints.
2. Trace each child's hands on a piece of paper. Cut out the shapes. These will be your cookie patterns.
3. Remove the chilled dough from the refrigerator, and roll it out in small sections on a floured surface. Make the dough about ¼ inch thick.
4. Put a handprint on the dough and cut out the shape with a knife. Repeat until all the handprints are cut out.
5. Put the cookies on lightly greased baking sheets. Bake at 375°F for 8 to 9 minutes until lightly browned.
6. Let the cookies completely cool on wire racks.
7. Make the icing by mixing a little water into the confectioners' sugar till you achieve spreading consistency. Add food coloring.
8. Ice the cookies and add candy decorations to your heart's desire!

VARIATIONS

3- to 4-Year-Olds

- Keep it simple. You can paint on the icing and let children add the decorations.

5- to 6-Year-Olds

- Make rings on the fingers, bracelets on the wrists, and knuckles.

7- to 9-Year-Olds

- Make plaid gloves; give your hands a manicure; match the right and left palms; even add a watch!

HINT

- Reroll the extra cookie dough. Shape it into a log and freeze it for slice-and-bake sugar cookies on another day.

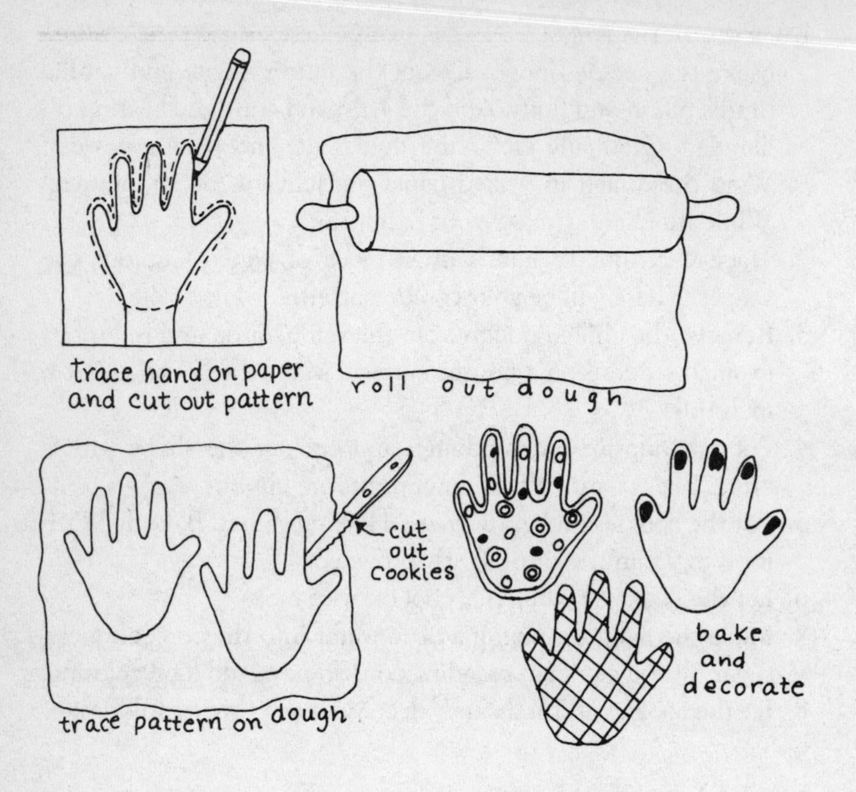
trace hand on paper
and cut out pattern
roll out dough
trace pattern on dough
cut
out
cookies
bake
and
decorate

Apple-on-a-Stick

Forget the gooey red-candy kind. These are apples for the Macintosh generation. Everywhere I take them, people stare and smile. The key is using tongue depressors for sticks . . . they're fun, sturdy, and easy to grasp.

INGREDIENTS

Apples
Tongue depressors
Paring knife

DIRECTIONS

1. Peel the apples.
2. Have your child stick the tongue depressor into the bottom stem end of the apple and push until the apple is steady. (You may need to help.)
3. Hold the apple like a popsicle and eat!

VARIATIONS

3- to 4-Year-Olds

- Try this with pears or any other hard fruit.

5- to 6-Year-Olds

- When your child has finished eating the apple, cut the core in half horizontally and look at the apple's "star."

7- to 9-Year-Olds

- Try doing this activity with bananas. Peel the banana, cut it in half, and put a stick in each piece. Cover the pieces with plastic wrap and freeze them. Eat the banana like an ice cream pop.

Chocolate-Covered Strawberries

Irresistible! Stacy Bogdonoff, a New York caterer, first showed me how to make these little delights for a dinner at our children's nursery school. I've been a fan of hers ever since.

MATERIALS

1 quart strawberries, as large as you can get
12-ounce bag of semisweet chocolate chips
Forks or bamboo skewers
Cookie pan or tray covered with waxed paper
Double boiler

DIRECTIONS

1. Wash the berries, but leave the stems on. Lay them on a paper towel to dry.
2. Prepare the chocolate. In order for it to stick, the chocolate must be tempered. This means you need to combine two extremes of temperature to reach a perfect middle. On the top of the stove or in a double boiler, melt three-quarters of the bag of chips. Stir the chocolate as it melts. Then, remove it from the heat and stir in the rest of the chips.
3. Have your child fork or skewer a strawberry from the stem end.
4. Dip the berry three-quarters of the way into the chocolate. Raise it up and put it on the waxed paper to cool.
5. When all the berries are done, place them in the refrigerator for half an hour.
6. Eat and enjoy!

VARIATIONS

3- to 4-Year-Olds

- Dip vanilla cookies, pretzels, or dried fruit.

5- to 6-Year-Olds

- Have ready a bowl of colored sprinkles. Quickly dip the chocolate-covered berries into the sprinkles.

7- to 9-Year-Olds

- Make multicolored chocolates. After you've dipped the dark chocolate, follow the same tempering instructions for white chocolate chips. Dip a fork in the melted white chocolate. Drizzle it over the dark berries. Cool and refrigerate.

HINT

- As complicated as tempering sounds, it's really easy. Don't skip that step and try to melt all the chocolate at once. It won't work.

QUIET TIMES

Crankiness before bed, irritability after lunch, arguments over nothing . . . these are just some of the difficulties that crop up every day. In our family we have "quiet time"—a cozy, cuddly, comfortable activity that makes us forget what all the commotion was about.

Read Me a Story

I read to them, they read to me, we all read to each other. A good book is worth reading again and again and again.

MATERIALS

A good book or two or four
Pillows to sit on

DIRECTIONS

1. Create a comfortable reading area. Put cushions on the floor or extra pillows on the sofa or bed.
2. Take turns choosing books, so each child gets one. Or, you pick for all.
3. Read together. If the story is familiar, pause and let the children tell you what's happening. Look at the pictures. Discuss events in your own life.
4. Let the older children read to the younger ones.

VARIATIONS

3- to 4-Year-Olds

- Let your child "read" a favorite story to you.

5- to 6-Year-Olds

- Find a chapter book and begin reading a chapter a night.

7- to 9-Year-Olds

- Even 9-year-olds still like to be read to. Pick a book that might be a little too hard for them to read themselves, but is still on their understanding level.
- Read nonfiction books.
- Look at maps and atlases.

HINTS

- Fairy tales, fables, holiday stories, and the classics are good for all ages.
- Nature books or books that explain how things work are also universally appealing.
- As you read, change your voice to fit the characters or mood of the book.

Growing Tall

I know you can buy growth charts, but it's much more personal when you make your own. Try putting this chart in the hallway between your children's rooms.

MATERIALS

A blank wall
Colored craft tape in 1-inch, ½-inch, and ¼-inch widths: You can buy this in art supply or hardware stores.
A yardstick
Markers
Pencil

DIRECTIONS

1. Clean the wall with household cleanser.
2. Position the yardstick on the floor, and lean it against the wall. Make light horizontal pencil lines at 2 feet and 3 feet; then connect them with a vertical line. With the ruler still in place, make horizontal lines every 2 inches between 2 feet and 3 feet.
3. Move the rule up and make marks at 4 feet and 5 feet. Make a vertical line from 5 feet to 3 feet. Again, mark every 2 inches with a light horizontal line.
4. Use the wide, 1" craft tape to create a tall vertical on the wall from 5 feet to 2 feet. Use the ½-inch tape to horizontally mark 2 feet, 2½ feet, 3 feet, 3½ feet, 4 feet, 4½ feet and 5 feet. Use the thinnest tape to mark the 2-inch intervals in between.
5. Stand each child against the wall; write the child's name and the date at the child's height.
6. If you have a record of your children's growth, mark those heights on your chart also.

VARIATIONS

3- to 4-Year-Olds

- Show your child how much he or she grew in a year.
- Show your child the height of an older sibling at 3 or 4 years of age.

5- to 6-Year-Olds

- Since this is usually a big growth spurt period, measure frequently!
- Have your children measure each other.

7- to 9-Year-Olds

- Figure out measurements in inches as well as feet.
- Convert measurements to centimeters.
- Subtract height differences: younger from older, last year's from this year's.

HINTS

- You may want to make your chart tall enough to measure Mom and Dad.
- If you don't have a wall to draw on, use a 3' x 6" piece of painted plywood.
- Add a weight measurement to each height and date entry.

Picture This

Children love to see photos . . . of yesterday or yesteryear. Whether it's your album or theirs, a picture *is* worth a thousand words.

MATERIALS

Family photo albums

DIRECTIONS

1. Sit down with your children, take out a photo album, and thumb through the pages.
2. Reminisce, reacquaint, explain, retell, and relive through pictures.

VARIATIONS

3- to 4-Year-Olds

- A baby book can also be used—theirs or yours!
- Pick out people who look like your child: you as a toddler, an older sibling at that age.

5- to 6-Year-Olds

- Find pictures of favorite parties or trips.
- Talk about what it feels like when you see yourself "little."

7- to 9-Year-Olds

- Find pictures from the beginning of school till now.
- Find pictures with lots of different expressions and discuss the feelings.

HINT

- It helps siblings understand each other when they see pictures of themselves at the age of a younger sibling . . . or see the older sib at the age they are now. It puts you in a new perspective when they see your baby pictures or wedding album.

Drawing Together

When we draw pictures together, I try to focus on a new skill. Even the youngest children appreciate learning to draw better.

MATERIALS

Drawing paper
Crayons, colored pencils, or oil pastels such as Cray-pas sticks
Pencils

DIRECTIONS

1. Give the children each a piece of paper. Decide what medium they will use and spread out the colors.
2. Together, set up a simple still life: a bowl of fruit; blocks; a toy train; shoes; a stuffed animal; or even a simple table lamp.
3. Help the children start to draw what they see.

VARIATIONS

3- to 4-Year-Olds

- Work with color and shape: For example, the blocks are squares; they're one on top of another; they're red, yellow, and blue.
- Trace your child's hand and have your child fill in the fingernails and knuckle lines.
- Teach your child how to make elbow and knee joints.

5- to 6-Year-Olds

- Work with color, shape, and proportion: For example, are some blocks bigger? In the fruit bowl, what's large and what's small?

- If you're using Cray-pas sticks or colored pencils, try blending colors.
- Focus on drawing legs and feet, or shoulders and arms.
- Teach your child how to draw a profile.

7- to 9-Year-Olds

- Teach perspective. Start with a simple cube shape and watch your child's fascination grow.
- Draw a room in perspective and show your child how things fit in.
- Look at books or photos that illustrate perspective.
- See how color can also be used for depth perception.
- Teach blending.
- Focus on drawing someone sitting or running.
- Try different media, such as charcoal. Try pencil shading.

HINT

- I keep small, professional sketch pads and a special set of Cray-pas sticks for these drawing sessions.

Letters on My Back

My own mom used to play this game with me. Now I often wake up my children this way . . . or lull them to sleep at night.

MATERIALS
None

DIRECTIONS
1. Have your child lie face down.
2. Gently rub your child's back. Then, using your index finger, trace a letter on her or his back. Have your child guess what letter you've written.

VARIATIONS
3- to 4-Year-Olds
- Stick to easy letters at first: *O, T, S,* or your child's initials.
- Use capital letters only.
- Use numbers.

5- to 6-Year-Olds
- Use lowercase letters or a combination of upper and lower.
- Use a feather, penny, Barbie doll, or toy car to write. Have the child guess what object you are using.

7- to 9-Year-Olds
- Play "Back Words." Make your letters into words. Have your child try to guess the words as well as the letters.

HINT
- This activity is another game that crosses all age lines. Let an older sib write on a younger child's back and vice versa. Let them try on you!

CAR TRIPS

We all know car rides can be murder. Everyone wants a window seat. Someone gets carsick. Another has to go to the bathroom. You missed the exit. And no one likes your radio station. The trick is planning several activities ahead of time, having a cache of coloring books and stickers, keeping emergency snacks in your glove compartment, and knowing when you really *must* stop for a break. Following are some fail-safe activities.

"I'm Thinking of Someone You Know"

A great guessing game.

MATERIALS
None

DIRECTIONS

1. Think of someone your children know. Then have each child ask a question about this person. You can answer only yes or no. For example:

   "Is this person a relative?" "Yes."
   "Is it a female?" "Yes."
   "Does she have red hair?" "No."

2. Whoever guesses the mystery person correctly wins the game and gets to be the next leader.

VARIATIONS

3- to 4-Year-Olds

- Pick very familiar people or objects—a teacher or a television character like Bert or Ernie from "Sesame Street" is a good start.
- Give your child hints on how to narrow down choices with questions. For example: Is it a relative? Is it a man? Do I see him every day?

5- to 6-Year-Olds

- Limit the number of questions you can ask to 20.

7- to 9-Year-Olds

- Limit the number of questions you can ask to 10.
- Play with categories such as historical figures, sports players, television characters.

HINT

- If your preschoolers are consistently outguessed by older siblings, take turns being the leader so everyone gets a chance.

License Plate ABC's

I sometimes even play this game when I'm all alone.

MATERIALS

None

DIRECTIONS

1. The first person picks any letter. The others must try to find that letter on a passing license plate.
2. Whoever finds the letter first, chooses the next letter.

VARIATIONS

3- to 4-Year-Olds

- Instead of choosing a letter, try to find the alphabet in order, looking on plates for an *A*, then a *B*, and continuing through the alphabet.
- Look for numbers in order: *0* to *9*.

5- to 6-Year-Olds

- Look for numbers in order from *0* to *20*.
- Use street signs and billboards to help you find your letters.

7- to 9-Year-Olds

- Think of words your child is learning to spell. Try to find either the word or the letters using license plates, signs, and billboards.
- Look for vanity plates or try to make up your own.
- Count how many different states you see license plates from.

Make a Tape

My kids are the only ones who love my singing. Not only do they listen to these tapes in the car, but we often play them during quiet times at home.

MATERIALS

Tape recorder
Blank tape
Favorite storybooks

DIRECTIONS

1. Set up the tape in the recorder.
2. Record yourself reading a child's favorite story.
3. Record your children singing some favorite songs. Have each child sing a verse or two.
4. Label the tape and put it in your car!

VARIATIONS

3- to 4-Year-Olds

- Sing with your children to get them started. Replay the recording so your children hear their voices. Then record some more.
- If there are parts of the book your child likes to repeat or read with you, include those on the tape.

5- to 6-Year-Olds

- Record riddles. Pause. Then give the answers.
- Let your child read part of a book.

7- to 9-Year-Olds

- Record a chapter book or a mystery. Pause so the children can try to guess the ending.

HINTS

- As I read, I often stop and ask questions—naming each child in the process. The kids get a real kick out of hearing me talking to them "on the radio."
- I try to read from beautiful picture books that I can later look at with my children.
- Lesser-known fairy tales seem to please all ages.

Car Bingo

This activity takes some up-front work, but it's easy and absorbing on the road.

MATERIALS

6 pieces of 8" x 11" cardboard to lean on: Have one for each person, plus one or two extra.
White paper
Ruler
Pencils
Markers

DIRECTIONS

1. Before your trip, make the bingo boards. On a piece of paper, make a list of 30 things you usually see on the road. A few ideas: stop sign, pickup truck, traffic light, convertible, yield sign, railroad crossing, gas station, Jeep.
2. With your ruler and markers, draw a grid—5 squares by 5 squares—on six separate sheets of white paper. Put an X in the center square.
3. On the first grid, write a different item from your list in each of the remaining 24 boxes. (You should have six items you didn't use.)
4. On the second grid, start with the six unused items and fill in those 24 boxes. Do this on all six grids. Each grid will be filled in in a different order.
5. To make a pack of game boards, photocopy the six grids several times each.

6. To play, give each player a different board (grid), a pencil, and a cardboard backing to lean on. Every time a player spots an item on the road that's also on his or her board, the player x's it out. The first player to x out an entire row—across, down, or diagonally—wins.

VARIATIONS

3- to 4-Year-Olds

- Draw pictures on your game boards instead of writing words.
- Use stickers as markers instead of pencils.

5- to 6-Year-Olds

- Play for distances: For example, see who gets the most *X*'s on a ride from home to Grandma's.

7- to 9-Year-Olds

- Play to fill an entire board.

HINT

- You can play in pairs. Match an older sibling with a younger one or play front seat against back.

Ten-Minute Stories

Once upon a time . . . our car rides didn't seem so endless.

MATERIALS
A stopwatch, or a car clock with a second hand

DIRECTIONS
1. Designate one timekeeper and one talker to begin.
2. The talker starts telling a story. It can be true or make-believe.
3. After 2 minutes, the timekeeper calls "Time!" and the talker stops—even in mid-sentence. The talker becomes the next timekeeper, and a new person becomes the talker.
4. After 2 minutes, you change again.
5. Keep talking and timing the story for 10 minutes, or five rounds. The last player to speak must conclude the plot.

VARIATIONS

3- to 4-Year-Olds
- Instead of timing, play so each person has two or three turns. Decide who will finish the plot.

5- to 6-Year-Olds
- Play with 1-minute talk times.
- Start with a familiar fairy tale and make a new ending.

7- to 9-Year-Olds
- The first person creates a mystery, and the next players must solve it within the 10-minute limit.
- Play for 20 minutes.

KID-SIZED JOBS

I'm a firm believer in having kids do chores around the house. Straightening a room, cleaning something, or organizing toys produces immediately apparent results. Even though having children do chores sometimes seems like more work for you, it's a good way to help your kids feel in control of their surroundings, involved, and productive.

Make a Menu

How many times have you said, "This is not a restaurant!" Well, pretend it is. Have your kids make a menu of what they'd like to eat and serve the *plat du jour* at each meal.

MATERIALS

8½" x 11" paper, lined
Pencils
Crayons

DIRECTIONS

1. Make a menu for each child. Fold the paper in half vertically.
2. Write "MENU" on the front.
3. Inside, write "Breakfast," "Lunch," "Dinner," "Drinks." Add "Desserts" and "Snacks" if these are important in your house. Depending upon how you plan to cook and serve, you can also subdivide into "Meats," "Vegetables," "Starches."
4. Have the children each list what they like to eat for every meal. They should have several choices under each heading.
5. At each meal, serve *one* of each child's choices.

VARIATIONS

3- to 4-Year-Olds

- You'll have to write down the choices, but your child—or you—can draw pictures next to the words.

5- to 6-Year-Olds

- Make it a game. Have the child name the restaurant and draw a picture on the cover.
- Talk about nutrition—what foods are good for you and why.

7- to 9-Year-Olds

- Discuss the food groups.
- Plan a special meal together.
- For fun, alphabetize the choices under each section.

HINT

- I use the menu for trouble meals. One of my daughters can never decide what to eat for breakfast. Her menu concentrates on breakfast choices. My son loves to choose the vegetables at dinner. His menu has a big veggie section. Empowering them with choices makes sure everyone gets something they like, and we all have a happy, healthy, interesting meal!

All Sorts of Things

Sorting things—toys, books, games—*can* be fun. The trick is making it a game instead of a task.

MATERIALS

Colored plastic containers, shoe boxes, bookends, buckets, or gift boxes

DIRECTIONS

1. Together, decide what you want to sort: Little People or Playmobile pieces, board games, books, trucks, Lego pieces, doll clothes, and sports equipment almost always need some reorganization.
2. Choose the perfect size container to put them in.
3. Work together until your child gets the knack!

VARIATIONS

3- to 4-Year-Olds

- Put the newly organized toys in accessible containers, and they'll be more likely to stay that way.
- Practice sorting when you unpack the groceries, fold the laundry, or empty the dishwasher.

5- to 6-Year-Olds

- Use mailing labels to label plastic containers. Write the article name in block letters and draw a picture of the contents next to it. (You could also take a Polaroid picture.) Now your child can "read" what's in each box.

7- to 9-Year-Olds

- Sort toys and books your child no longer plays with and can hand down to a younger sibling.
- Sort school papers and artwork that you want to save. Put them in a cardboard portfolio.

Ready, Set, Eat

It's never too early to learn how to set the table. This activity also has the advantages of teaching right and left, and table manners.

MATERIALS
Spoons, forks, and knives
Napkins
Plates
Glasses

DIRECTIONS

1. Arrange a standard place setting: fork and napkin on the left, spoon and knife and glass on the right. Explain where and how everything goes (for example, the knife on the inside, the napkin folded in). Have your child arrange a setting next to yours.
2. Have your child set the table for the family.

VARIATIONS

3- to 4-Year-Olds

- Make a place-setting place mat for your child. Put it under your child's plate. Your children can refer to it when setting the table.
- Let your child set just the napkins, or just the forks. Gradually work up to the entire place setting.

5- to 6-Year-Olds

- Include centerpieces on your table. Try flowers, dolls, a train car, fruit, candlesticks, or anything else you can think of.
- Experiment with folding the napkins different ways: triangles, rectangles, squares.

7- to 9-Year-Olds

- Introduce soup spoons and dessert or salad forks. Show your children where these go and when they are used. Do the same thing with different-sized plates.
- Make napkin rings out of pipe cleaners and use them to decorate the table.

HINT

- I always try to include a child's touch on my holiday dinner tables. Whether it's folding the napkins, placing the silverware, or arranging the flowers, everyone helps make the table perfect.

Washing the Car

Washing the car is a "legal" way to play with water. If only kids thought washing themselves were as much fun!

MATERIALS

A car
Buckets of soapy water: Liquid dishwashing detergent is ideal and mild.
Large sponges for washing
Rags for drying
A hose
Window cleaner for inside
Portable, handheld vacuum cleaner

DIRECTIONS

1. Soap up the outside.
2. Hose it off!
3. Wipe the inside with rags and window cleaner.
4. Vacuum the seats and floor.
5. Stand back and admire your work.

VARIATIONS

3- to 4-Year-Olds

- Assign specific parts—such as tires or doors—that they can reach and complete.
- Hosing is easy and immediately gratifying.

5- to 6-Year-Olds

- Work in teams: One washes, one hoses. Switch jobs halfway through.
- Use a squeegee on the outside windows.

7- to 9-Year-Olds

- Washing the inside requires more care and less water. Assign it to an older child.
- Waxing the car is another harder task, but even that can be fun.
- When you're done washing, play catch with the wet sponges!

HINTS

- A car wash can easily turn into a bike wash or a swing-set wash or an outdoor-furniture wash. As long as you're wet and soapy, go to it!
- On hot days, wear a bathing suit.

Ready to Redecorate

Changing a child's room usually means the child is ready for a new stage of life. It could be as momentous as entering kindergarten or as simple as moving into spring. Likewise, redecorating can mean changing everything from furniture to carpets to curtains, or it can mean merely updating the artwork on the walls. As with adults, some kids want to redecorate whenever they can. Some will do it only once in 5 years. Some children hate any change at all. The key is involving your child in the process. A child who feels that she or he helped solve a problem has an investment in the solution.

MATERIALS

A "needy" room

DIRECTIONS

1. Determine the scope of your redecorating. Is it cosmetic or functional—does your child now need a desk for homework or just suddenly want the sheets to be lavender?
2. Make a plan of action determining what you want to achieve; what stays and what goes; and what new items you may need to buy.
3. Work together. Experiment. Move furniture. Use towels, sheets, or even shirts to see how new colors will look in the room. Squint. Look at magazines. Encourage individuality!

VARIATIONS

3- to 4-Year-Olds

- Character sheets or linens in a favorite color are always a boost.
- Reachable clothes hooks mean your child can dress and undress independently.
- Stackable toy bins remove clutter and leave more space for play.

5- to 6-Year-Olds

- A change of artwork is always a good time to see how much improvement has occurred since the first pictures were done.
- A beanbag chair, a chair that flips open to make a bed, or a cluster of throw pillows can create a perfect reading corner.

7- to 9-Year-Olds

- A homework file, a desk set, a grown-up lamp give credibility to this new level of student.
- Bed linens that mix solids and prints are totally sophisticated.
- Throw pillows or bolsters create a cozy place to talk with friends or read.

HINTS

- Think about adding a wall border. It's inexpensive and can pull a whole room together. You can paint, wallpaper, or even stencil one yourself.
- I always redecorate at the end of the summer. Having a new space to focus on often alleviates some of the anxiety of facing a new grade. It also helps the children express what they think their needs will be.
- When two children share a room, help them work out the plan together. If each has a favorite color, find fabric or paper that will coordinate with both. However, if, for example, one loves fire engines and one loves Disney characters, choose a neutral color scheme and hang framed photos of their choice over each bed. And most importantly, even though it's shared space, make sure each child has a "private" area within the room for his or her special toys or collections.

index

About the Author

While successfully juggling a variety of preschool, after-school, and in-school activities, Wendy Smolen is a full-time magazine editor, a corporate wife, and the mother of three young children. Throughout her career, she has worked as the creative director of two major cosmetic companies, has published articles in *Parents, Victoria, Mademoiselle, Harper's Bazaar,* and other magazines and has written advertising, catalogs, press releases, and videos for clients ranging from seed companies to high-fashion stores. She lives in New York City with her husband Paul and children Dana, Riki, and Zak.

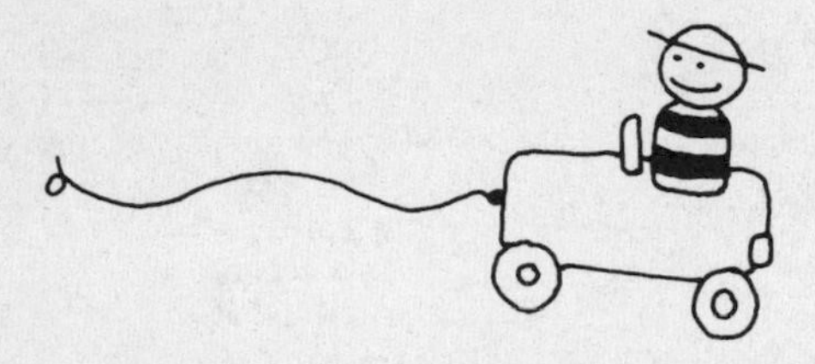